MINI COOPER
1961–2000

Peter Barker

AMBERLEY

To my family and friends who have tolerated my Mini Cooper obsession over the last forty years.

Cover images:
Mini Cooper in the snow. The author with Willy Cave hard at work during the 2008 Rallye Monte-Carlo Historique. (Phillipe Fugier)

The author with Willy Cave as they tackle the dreaded Col de l'Écharasson during the 2007 Rallye Monte-Carlo Historique. (Francois Haase)

A perfect Christmas scene: Mini Cooper 977ARX hurrying down the Col de Menée during the 2008 Rallye Monte-Carlo Historique. (Philippe Fugier)

1967 Rallye Monte-Carlo. The winning works Mini Cooper S of Rauno Aaltonen and Henry Liddon (car 177) alongside that of Simo Lampinen and Mike Wood, who finished fifteenth overall at a service point. (McKlein)

An early photo of the author, aged two, with his father's MiniVan. (Peter Barker)

First published 2021

Amberley Publishing
The Hill, Stroud
Gloucestershire, GL5 4EP

www.amberley-books.com

Copyright © Peter Barker, 2021

The right of Peter Barker to be identified as the Author of this work has been asserted in accordance with the Copyrights, Designs and Patents Act 1988.

ISBN 978 1 3981 0340 5 (print)
ISBN 978 1 3981 0341 2 (ebook)

British Library Cataloguing in Publication Data.
A catalogue record for this book is available from the British Library.

Typeset in 10pt on 13pt Celeste.
Typesetting by SJmagic DESIGN SERVICES, India.
Printed in Great Britain.

Contents

Acknowledgements

Firstly thank you to Amberley Publishing for publishing this book and for their encouragement. To the successive editors of *MiniWorld* magazine between 1994 and 2012, Mike Askew, Monty Watkins and Karen Drury, I must say a big thank you for facilitating and publishing historical articles plus over fifty of my interviews with people involved in the development and enjoyment of the Mini and Mini Cooper. Added to other historical articles published in the Mini Cooper Register's magazine (thanks to editors Lesley Young and Paul Sulma), a large body of knowledge was accumulated, which has been accessed for this book. Officers and members of the Mini Cooper Register have also been helpful with historical information and with images of their own. The owners and staff of SMMC are to be thanked and recommended for their unfailing expertise and efficiency as top Mini Cooper engineers. To all of those I have interviewed and quoted (some sadly no longer living) thank you for your patience, it was a privilege to spend time with you. Finally, the biggest thank you of all goes to Alec Issigonis and John Cooper for conceiving of the Mini Cooper in the first place.

Introduction

With the benefit of sixty years of hindsight it is possible to see that the introduction of the first Mini Cooper in 1961 was the start of something big. More than just a tuned up small car (after all there were tuned versions of the Austin Seven as long ago as the early 1920s), the Mini Cooper was the first British production vehicle in which the names of a major manufacturer (Austin and Morris) were twinned with that of a top-flight racing car constructor (the Cooper Car Company) to mutual benefit. Other manufacturers followed suit (Ford and Lotus, Vauxhall and Brabham) but the Mini Cooper remained out in front both in terms of sales and of influence. Hot hatches from VW, Peugeot and others came and went during the later twentieth century and there are many performance versions of small family cars on the market today. However, all these automotive phenomena can claim to have been started by the Mini Cooper.

A typical second-generation owner, I bought my first Mini Cooper as a young student of engineering in 1982, a 998cc Austin Cooper in Island blue and Snowberry white with 77,000 miles on the clock. Already fourteen years old, it had been pretty well used, but it introduced me to sportscar handling and lively performance (once I had learned how to dismantle and rebuild the engine). It also introduced me to road rallying, which was a highly affordable and popular branch of motorsport in those days.

For many people like me the Mini Cooper was an introduction to motoring and to motorsport. Both of those activities have given great pleasure to myself and successive generations of people at the steering wheel of their Mini Coopers. For that we should say a collective 'thank you'!

Chapter 1
A Car for the Boys (and Girls)

In a BBC TV interview filmed during the 1960s Alec Issigonis, designer of the Mini for manufacturers the British Motor Corporation, usually referred to as BMC, explained how a conversation with his friend and racing car designer John Cooper set in motion the development of the Mini Cooper:

> I am indebted very much to my old friend John Cooper who came along to see me one day and he said to me 'this little family car that you have designed is fantastic'. And I said to John 'But why is it fantastic?' But he said to me 'Have you taken it round a racing circuit?' I said 'No, should I have done? It's a people's car, I built it for them to go shopping and on holiday. I designed it for the district nurse really you know.' 'So why did you make it handle so well?' 'So that they were comfortable driving, so that they felt happy driving the car'. He said 'You haven't built a people's car you've built a racing car! We ought to build some of these for the boys, you know a little better, bit more steam, better brakes and better finish inside'.

Whether this conversation between Issigonis and Cooper is fact or was a product of Issigonis's fertile imagination, between them in early 1960 these two men conceived of a whole new phenomenon: the Mini Cooper. By marrying the sporting name and engine development abilities of World Championship-winning Formula 1 team the Cooper Car Company with the outstanding roadholding and cornering abilities of Issigonis's Mini a new and instantly appealing automotive product was born. At their launch on 26 August 1959 the new 850cc Austin Seven and Morris Mini Minor models, differently named to preserve marque allegiances among potential buyers, had been highly praised by the

Alec Issigonis as interviewed for BBC TV. (BMC)

world's motoring journalists. In its review of the new car *The Motor*, a leading automotive journal of the day, commented in formal tones:

> ...the new Austin Seven ... offers a remarkable combination of speed with economy, roominess with compactness and controllability with comfort.

In fact it was the perfect small car. The Mini had been designed to embody as much primary safety (the capacity of the car to adhere to the road and to be controllable by its driver under extreme conditions) as possible. In this it was very successful, even more so than its designers had anticipated. The handling of this tiny new car was so outstanding it could easily handle more power but that had never been the original design intention. In the words of the Mini's suspension engineer Dr Alex Moulton,

> The irony of it is of course that the astonishing behaviour of the Mini was picked up so splendidly by John Cooper in making a sports version of the thing, was not intended as a sporting thing at all. Simply our preoccupation was with the safe behaviour, our concern was with safety, safety, safety of handling and having given it that safety of handling it was then others like John Cooper who thought we can make this thing twitch about and be a wonderful little sportscar.

At that time the Cooper Car Company were at the top of their game as far as Formula 1 design and construction were considered, having won both the Formula 1 Constructor's Championship and Driver's Championship in 1959 and 1960. However, with up-and-coming

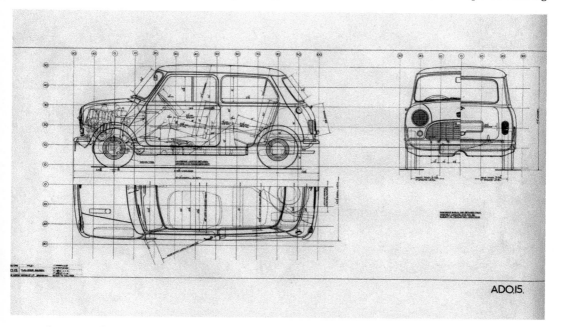

ADO.15.

The astonishingly compact packaging of the Mini is shown here in this beautiful drawing from 1959. Still shown here under its codename ADO15, the Mini was launched in the same year to a mixed reception. However, the Mini Cooper was a sales success from the word go. (BMC)

Dr Alex Moulton (1920–2012) was the inventor of the Mini Cooper's suspension systems, both rubber cone and fluid-filled Hydrolastic. An outstanding conceptual engineer, Alex Moulton worked with Alec Issigonis on the design of the Mini and Mini Cooper among several other models for BMC. (Alex Moulton Charitable Trust)

John Cooper (on the right with the bottle) celebrates Jack Brabham's win in a Cooper GP single seat racing car at the 1959 US Grand Prix. (McKlein)

rivals such as Colin Chapman's Lotus team hard on their heels for 1961 and beyond it was going to be difficult for John Cooper's small Surbiton-based team to win the championship for a third time. A diversification into sporting road cars was timely and capitalised nicely upon Cooper's recent success. Despite Issigonis's lukewarm attitude to the idea of making a sporting version of his new baby car, John Cooper and his chief engineer 'Ginger' Devlin borrowed an early Mini and set about improving it.

Out went the Mini's BMC 848cc A series engine and gearbox with its accompanying 'magic wand' gearstick. In went a 'Cooperised' long-stroke 997cc A series engine with closer gear ratios (four forward speeds and one reverse as previously), plus an all-new remote gear change mechanism. This mechanism with its short chrome-plated gearstick and black plastic gear knob transformed gearchanges as it bought the stick much closer to the driver's seating position. This sped up the whole process of changing gear (an activity the sporting driver was going to be doing a great deal of it was thought) and made it more accurate. In turn this put less stress and wear on the gearbox components. The new engine put out 'more steam' as John Cooper had wished. A healthy 55 bhp (brake horsepower, the contemporary measurement of engine power) in fact compared with the 848cc Mini's 34 bhp. The free-breathing new Cooper engine revved easily to peak power at 6,000 rpm (revs per minute) whereas the less powerful Mini engine's power peaked a whole 1,000 rpm lower.

With more power from the engine the 'better brakes' wished for were also fitted. John Cooper spoke to his friend Jack Emmot, whose company Lockheed had been working on a miniature disc brake layout as an experimental item. These tiny 7-inch discs with their puny calipers were fitted to the prototype Mini Cooper, making it the first small production car to be fitted with disc brakes. Dunlop Gold-Seal tyres in the standard Mini's size of 5.20 inches x 10 inches were fitted to 3.5-inch J section painted steel wheels, which were themselves fitted with smart looking polished stainless steel hubcaps.

The exterior of this first Mini Cooper was treated to a dual colour paint job (the roof panel in black contrasting with the grey body colour) and chromed trim around the front windows. A new and distinctive radiator grille graced the front of the car and highly desirable badges were made, proudly announcing the car's name on the bonnet and boot lid. Inside the car new two-tone vinyl upholstery was fitted and little chromed door levers replaced the string pulls of the standard Mini. A swathe of black vinyl across the dash rail and up the inside of the A pillars completed the new interior. A new 100 mph speedometer with gearchange markings, plus water temperature and oil pressure gauges in a widened black vinyl dash pod, gave the driver a little more information on the health of the car. The whole package looked smart and sporting. With its two-tone paint and new brightwork the

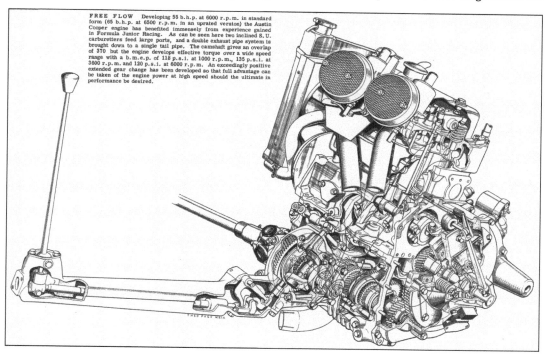

FREE FLOW Developing 55 b.h.p. at 6000 r.p.m. in standard form (65 b.h.p. at 6500 r.p.m. in an uprated version) the Austin Cooper engine has benefited immensely from experience gained in Formula Junior Racing. As can be seen here two inclined S. U. carburetters feed large ports, and a double exhaust pipe system is brought down to a single tail pipe. The camshaft gives an overlap of 370 but the engine develops effective torque over a wide speed range with a b.m.e.p. of 118 p.s.i. at 1000 r.p.m., 135 p.s.i. at 3600 r.p.m. and 120 p.s.i. at 6000 r.p.m. An exceedingly positive extended gear change has been developed so that full advantage can be taken of the engine power at high speed should the ultimate in performance be desired.

The Mini Cooper engine and gearbox unit for launch during 1961. This superb cutaway drawing by Theo Page shows the new power unit in all its glory. (BMC)

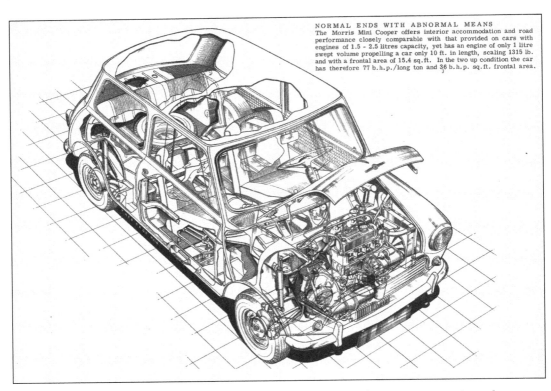

NORMAL ENDS WITH ABNORMAL MEANS
The Morris Mini Cooper offers interior accommodation and road
performance closely comparable with that provided on cars with
engines of 1.5 - 2.5 litres capacity, yet has an engine of only 1 litre
swept volume propelling a car only 10 ft. in length, scaling 1315 lb.
and with a frontal area of 15.4 sq.ft. In the two up condition the car
has therefore 77 b.h.p./long ton and 36 b.h.p. sq.ft. frontal area.

Morris Mini Cooper cutaway drawing from 1961 by Theo Page. Such a compact sporting saloon
had never been produced before and BMC were rightly very proud of it. (BMC)

Mini Cooper was distinctive enough from the Mini to stand out on the road and attracted
as many admiring glances as its driver could wish for.

However, the acid test for the new sports saloon car was how it performed. On a wet and
gloomy day at the Silverstone Grand Prix circuit Issigonis was presented with the prototype
Mini Cooper and a standard Mini to try out. When it became clear that the Cooper version
of the Mini was two seconds a lap quicker around the circuit, he gave the project his
support. Together with John Cooper he approached Sir George Harriman, chairman of the
board of directors at BMC and asked for the new car to be put into production.

By all accounts Sir George was reluctant to do so as at the time (1960) sales of the
standard Mini had not yet taken off sufficiently to see any prospect of a return on BMC's
considerable investment in putting the little car into production. However, John Cooper
was nothing if not persuasive and after a test drive in the prototype Harriman committed
to production of 1,000 cars (the minimum number needed to allow the car to be entered
in production saloon car racing). He also agreed on a £2 royalty per car produced for John
Cooper, which must have seemed a steal with only 1,000 cars to be made. By 1971 with over
100,000 cars produced that didn't seem such a good deal to future management but that's
another story!

Inside BMC the still secret new car was given the project designation ADO50. ADO
allegedly either stood for Austin Drawing Office or Amalgamated Drawing Office depending
upon who you spoke to, and 50 was the next free number in a series. Development of

The prototype Austin Mini Cooper pictured with its creator John Cooper (in the dark top) and a Cooper Formula 1 car. The new Mini Cooper is finished in grey and black, which was not a colour ever offered to the public, and is without its Cooper badging. The car is otherwise pretty much as sold to the public from September 1961. (*MiniWorld* archive)

ADO50 took place during the autumn of 1960 with a projected date of reveal to the press set on 17 July 1961 and sales to the public from September of that year. Progress was hampered both by internal wrangling within BMC and problems with the supply of special parts required for the new Mini Cooper. By 17 July BMC had only managed to build ten examples of the new model to present to the press at Chobham test track. The pre-launch dinner was held at the Kensington Palace Hotel in London the evening before and no fewer than twenty-seven Grand Prix drivers were listed as guests. Clearly BMC were keen to stress the new Mini Cooper's racing heritage. Issigonis presided over the ceremonies and must have enjoyed the company of so many talented drivers.

Next day the world's motoring press, summoned to Chobham this time not only to enjoy the brilliant handling of Issigonis's little car but now given enough power to make it fun, reveled in the drivability of the new Mini Cooper. Peter Merritt, writing in the *Aberdeen Evening Express* subsequently, was typical of many:

What happens when Cooper's championship-winning quality is added to the Mini is enough to send even the most blasé motorist into raptures of enthusiasm. Many drivers will want to drive this car hard and fast. Even so, fuel consumption should remain well [on] the right side of 30 mpg. The car is fast but it is also very safe.

BMC's own press pack, issued to journalists on the day, ended its copy with this phrase:

The Austin Cooper commands the respect of those who observe it and arouses the affection of those who drive it. It not only takes you but it also sends you.

Powerful words and unusually for PR information completely true and accurate.

Chapter 2
'The Ten Foot Tornado'

It was F. Wilson McComb, the editor of the MG Car Club's magazine *Safety Fast*, who coined the phrase 'The Ten Foot Tornado' when reviewing the Austin and Morris Coopers. The original 997cc Mini Cooper was well received by its buyers, racing and rally drivers and journalists alike as it gave the Mini what it desperately needed: more power. The handling of the car was as good as the original Mini despite a little more weight and roadholding was better thanks to the new Dunlop Gold Seal tyres. Even more was to come in this department as after three years of production Dunlop introduced radial tyres for the Mini Cooper's 10-inch wheels, which became standard fit from March 1964. These little radials (either SP41 for the road or SP3 with its more open tread for rally drivers) transformed the grip level available to the Mini Cooper, making it practically unbeatable on twisty roads.

The new Mini Cooper was launched in a wonderful array of duotone contemporary colour schemes, body colour with a contrasting white or black roof. However, what was to become the iconic Mini Cooper colour scheme of Tartan red with an Old English white roof was not actually one of them. That came later through works competition use. The interior of the car was treated with the most eye-catching (or garish depending upon your point of view) multitone vinyl coverings, some having either a sliver or gold inlay, which varied with car body colour and model year. Issigonis's little box was looking sumptuous and any idea of austerity being associated with the Mini Cooper was quietly forgotten. The new Mini Cooper sold at £679 in the UK, which included a purchase tax loading of no less than £314 (46 per cent). In twenty-first-century Britain

A very early Austin Cooper still with its 997cc engine. Although superficially modified, this Almond green and Old English white car was fundamentally original and had only passed through the hands of two owners when it was photographed in 2006. (Peter Barker)

we complain about VAT, which is set at 20 per cent at the time of writing; 46 per cent tax is simply hideous!

As the public were already familiar with the basic layout of the car there was none of the hesitancy that buyers had displayed directly following the launch of the Mini in 1959. Sales took off instantly. Although sales to the public only began in September 1961, by the end of that year the 1,000 cars originally produced had already been sold, with another 128 cars sold in the UK market. A further 647 cars had been sent abroad by the end of 1961 and in 1962 sales rocketed, with 7,254 cars sold in the UK and 6,710 abroad. BMC's directors must have been very happy with their little gamble on the Cooper name.

Everyone seemed to fall in love with the Mini Cooper from the word go, from professional race and rally drivers to ordinary owners who bought a 'Cooper', as they inevitably became known, for daily transport. Here was a small sporting car that was genuinely practical at the same time. With its 90-mph performance and excellent handling it outperformed many contemporary sportscars and could accommodate a family of four or even five at a squeeze. What wasn't there to like about it?

Well, the brakes for one thing. The tiny disc brakes with their diminutive brake calipers soon overheated when faced with the kind of spirited driving a Mini Cooper provoked. Many complaints were made and the engineers at Longbridge, BMC's development facility and main manufacturing plant in Birmingham, soon improved the brake master cylinder, as well as the front brake calipers and pads. Even with these improvements braking was marginal. The author can attest to the poor braking power of an early Mini Cooper as he had to take to a field to avoid disaster during a night road rally in Wales, the early brakes disappearing when they were needed most!

Synchromesh on the early Mini Cooper gearbox was also an issue. The cones that meshed gears together soon wore out given the extra power of the new car and the frequent gear changes it encouraged. In the summer of 1962 the cone type synchromesh was replaced by baulk ring synchromesh, which solved this problem, although there were others with the gearbox that were not finally cured until the replacement of the A type gears with B type gears in March 1963.

In early 1964, by which time 24,860 Mini Coopers had been produced, the long stroke 997cc engine was replaced by a short stroke 998cc unit. This new version of BMC's A series engine had been pioneered in the Mini variant Riley Elf and Wolseley Hornet models, and was given a tune-up for introduction in the Mini Cooper. A new cylinder head with part number 12G295 was fitted to most 998 Coopers (as they became known) and this revolutionary casting benefitted from the latest in combustion chamber and port design. In standard form it was good and given a little tuning work it became the cylinder head of choice for any sub-1,000cc A series engine. Power was boosted by only 1 bhp against the 997 engine but the capacity for revs was greatly increased by the new engine's short stroke, which bought with it a host of tuning possibilities. The 998cc engine made the Mini Cooper easier to drive and more docile on the road while offering the enthusiast the promise of extra power at relatively little cost. In John Cooper's words 'the 998cc engine was the right Cooper engine for the man in the street'.

Presumably this also applied to the woman in the street as a sizable proportion of Mini Cooper sales were being made to women, particularly young women, for whom it was

1966 registered Morris Cooper in Almond green and Old English white colours. As manufactured the car would have been fitted with stainless steel hubcaps, a white plastic backed rearview mirror and an unheated windscreen. Otherwise it appears to be in standard trim. (Peter Barker)

a perfect first car. Carol Beynon moved from England to Germany to work in the British Embassy in Bonn, and she took her new Mini Cooper with her.

> I'd actually only just passed my driving test and had ordered a new 1,000cc Mini Cooper tax free to take with me. I started off by learning the finer points of driving in the Exiles Car Club, taking part in treasure hunts, driving tests and so on. This whet my appetite and I started entering proper German rallies and working my way up to national events.

Not every Mini Cooper was driven quite so hard by their owners, but many seemed to gravitate that way. Drivers just couldn't help but enjoy the performance of the little car and many people such as Carol used their road cars for a bit of amateur motorsport. The Mini Cooper probably did as much for improved driving standards as any model of car before or since. It enabled perfectly ordinary road users to experience precise car control and decent performance, luxuries which had hitherto been the preserve of racing drivers only.

The entire Mini saloon family was treated to Moulton-patented Hydrolastic suspension in 1964, which gave the car a more supple ride. Not universally popular in a Mini as it caused highly variable pitch angles under acceleration and braking, Hydrolastic was eventually banned on cars exported to Germany as it sent headlamp beams pointing skyward when the car was accelerating hard and/or heavily loaded.

In late 1967 the entire Mini range was given a makeover with a different grille design, revised badges, squared off lamps at the rear, new colour schemes and a host of interior

Above: Carol Beynon (left) and her sponsor display their racing trophies on the bonnet of Carol's well used 1968 Morris Mini Cooper. (*MiniWorld* archive)

Right: A sectioned Moulton-Dunlop Hydrolastic unit shows the rubber 'cheese' and upper and lower fluid reservoirs, as well as the valve that controlled fluid movement. Two of these units were interconnected on each side of the car, giving a supple and stable ride. (Alex Moulton Charitable Trust)

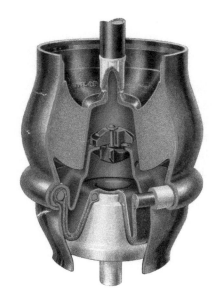

improvements. The new range was known as the Mk2 Mini and the Mini Cooper was no exception. Inside the car the trim was simplified and offered in black only. A headlamp flasher was fitted to the new steering column mounted indicator/horn stalk. Mk1 Minis had a floor-mounted headlamp dipping switch that was far from convenient. Electrical items, steering lock and safety features were all improved and the new Mk2 Mini Cooper felt much more modern to drive that its predecessor. Radial tyres, which had been fitted as standard to the 998 Cooper since 1964, combined with Hydrolastic suspension to give the Mini Cooper excellent levels of grip and a comfortable ride.

Production of the 998cc Mini Cooper continued full scale until 1969 when the Mini Cooper was suddenly terminated by new owners British Leyland. A further 145 cars were made in 1970 to use up the stock of parts, which brought total production of the Mk1 and Mk2 Mini Coopers to 106,256.

Missing its hinged rear number plate (a device to allow the car to be driven legally with the boot open), this late registered Mk2 Mini Cooper S in Island blue and Snowberry white displays many of the minor modifications typical of its day including door-mounted wing mirrors and reversing light. (Peter Barker)

Chapter 3
A Real One: Mini Cooper S 1071, 970 and 1275

With the Mini Cooper selling well by mid-1962, John Cooper felt bold enough to approach BMC again in a bid for more performance for the little saloon car that bore his name. The Cooper Car Co. was competitive in Formula Junior racing based upon single seater cars with a maximum engine capacity of 1,100cc. Having used the BMC A series as his preferred engine in this formula since 1959, John Cooper and his team knew a lot about modifying the engine within its 1,100cc limit. As the 1,100cc limit also applied to saloon car racing at that time John Cooper proposed an improved Mini Cooper with a 1,100cc engine and better brakes. Between the Cooper Car Co. and BMC's engines branch in Coventry (known locally as 'Morris Motors') a 1,071cc version of the A series engine was developed. This featured a new cylinder head, influenced by Downton Engineering and coded AEG163, much improved crankshaft, connecting rod and piston assemblies and (for sale to the public) a milder camshaft profile than the contemporary 997cc Mini Cooper. Larger 7.5-inch-diameter (190 mm) front disc brakes were fitted with greatly improved brake calipers and pads. For the first time on any Mini a Lockheed brake servo was fitted. A wider track was achieved by the use of new special ventilated steel wheels (either 3.5J or at extra cost 4.5J section) and wheel spacers or later modified brake drums at the rear. The

The very first Austin Cooper S to be registered, 731HOP shows off its 1,071cc power at Brands Hatch. An adoring public bought as many Cooper S models as could be made once the motorsport successes started to flow. (*MiniWorld* archive)

new engine produced 70 bhp, which gave the car a top speed close to 100 mph, and the brakes were more than adequate for the car's greatly enhanced performance.

This little hot-rod, introduced in April 1963, was named the Mini Cooper S (S for sport or special) and was once again an instant success. Immediately entered into races and rallies by Cooper and BMC respectively, the Mini Cooper S took Warwick Banks to overall victory in the European Touring Car Championship and Paddy Hopkirk to the Mini Cooper's most famous rally victory, an outright win (on handicap it must be said) in the 1964 Rallye Monte-Carlo, 'the Monte' in British parlance. With the introduction of the Mini Cooper S the Mini Cooper went from fame to stardom. Suddenly it was the car to be seen in, especially in London where its diminutive size and startling performance were perfect for the city's narrow streets and (by 1963 standards) heavy traffic. Celebrities such as Paul McCartney, Peter Sellers, Marianne Faithfull and George Harrison were all seen zipping around London in their Mini Cooper S models. Steve McQueen and Enzo Ferrari used their 'pocket rockets' back home in the United States and Italy respectively to similar effect, encouraging overseas sales at the same time.

Still not content and with the 1,071cc Mini Cooper S having won rallies and races outright, John Cooper took another trip to visit BMC's board of directors at Longbridge. He once again worked his magic and persuaded the board, initially against their will, to produce two new versions of the Mini Cooper S. The ultimate large engined version, the famous '1275', was specifically aimed at the new 1,300cc class in racing and rallying. This car was, in John Cooper's reported words 'a real one' and would additionally replace

In practically standard condition (a rarity among Mini Coopers) this early Austin Cooper S, in Tartan red and black, shows off its narrow 3.5 inch J ventilated steel wheels. Apart from a windscreen-mounted GPS unit, the interior of the car looks standard. Even the original 'bus driver' large diameter steering wheel is in place. (Peter Barker)

the 1,071cc Mini Cooper S for the road. Production of the 1,071cc engine accordingly ceased in 1964 after 4,031 cars had been built. A smaller 970cc engine version aimed specifically at the 1,000cc racing class was to be produced to homologation (qualifying) production numbers only. This version too was out of production by the end of 1965 by which time 963 cars equipped with it had been completed. Cooper's new 1,275cc engine gave the Mini Cooper S 75 bhp and for the first time a genuine 100 mph top speed. BMC, Dunlop and Moulton Developments soon realised that a Mini with as much performance as the new 1,275cc Mini Cooper S needed uprated suspension. At a suspension meeting held on 2 September 1964 in Coventry it was agreed that special Hydrolastic units for the Mini Cooper S should be produced with harder rubber components and optimised fluid flow characteristics. These were fitted to cars on the production line as soon as the displacers became available. In time a variety of different Hydrolastic units became available principally for the Mini Cooper S, although they could be retrofitted to other Hydrolastic suspended Mini models. Identified by different coloured bands painted around the shells of the displacers, even stiffer and harder units intended for rallying and racing respectively could be purchased through BMC Special Tuning.

The promise of 100-mph performance from a four-seater car that was only 10 feet (2.54 metres) long was enough for wealthy buyers to pay around twice the price of a standard Mini for the Mini Cooper S. Soon the police forces of Britain found that they too had to get in on the Mini Cooper S act on the basis that you needed one to catch one. The Mini Cooper S also had a decent carrying capacity for police gear unlike some of the contemporary sportscars that equaled its performance.

By now a burgeoning aftermarket spares and tuning industry for the Mini Cooper had developed in Britain and elsewhere. Undoubtedly top of the tuning tree was Downton Engineering, founded by the highly talented if eccentric Daniel Richmond and his formidable wife Bunty. Well established and even more well connected in social circles, Downton Engineering was in the prefect position to benefit from the Mini Cooper

The Downton Engineering-modified Mini Cooper S 777MCG shown here in Central London in 1963. Sporting a set of Cooper 'Rosepetal' alloy wheels and what look like racing tyres, this car, modified by the genius of Daniel Richmond and others, would have been an extremely potent vehicle around town. (*MiniWorld* archive)

phenomenon. Daniel Richmond's forte was in understanding the flow of fuel/air mixture through the induction manifolds, cylinder head and gas through the exhaust system of an A series engine. Richmond developed two new cylinder heads which came to be produced as castings 12G295 for the 998 Cooper and 12G163 for the early Cooper S. A later development for the 1275 Cooper S, casting 12G940, was more reliable than the earlier cylinder head and versions of this later cylinder head were used on 1,275cc A series engines up until the end of production in 2000. Downton's consultancy royalties on the design and development of cylinder heads for BMC engines were such that Daniel Richmond was able to effectively retire and concentrate on salmon fishing, his other passion, until his early death in 1974.

Less flamboyant than Downton Engineering, a whole host of vehicle engineers and tuners developed parts and accessories for the Mini Cooper and Cooper S. Alexander Engineering, Derrington, Janspeed, Nerus and Taurus among many others sold 'conversions' for the Mini Cooper S, making a fast car even faster. It seemed that no Mini Cooper S survived long after leaving the factory before it succumbed to the attentions of one tuner or another. A standard Mini Cooper of any type became hard to find. Customisation or personalisation became 'de rigeur' for all Cooper owners, establishing a trend of customising small cars that continues to this day.

In 1964 BMC themselves got in on the tuning act with the establishment of the Special Tuning department at Abingdon. Closely allied to the Competitions Department and situated next door to it, BMC Special Tuning, under the management of sportscar specialist Basil Wales, sold tuning parts to BMC customers who wanted more performance from their everyday cars. Later on they tuned customers cars for them particularly if promotional race or rally use was intended. Initially aimed at offsetting the expense of running the BMC Competitions Department, Special Tuning was profitable, although the income it generated never equaled BMC's outlay on factory-backed competitions. Special Tuning offered a very

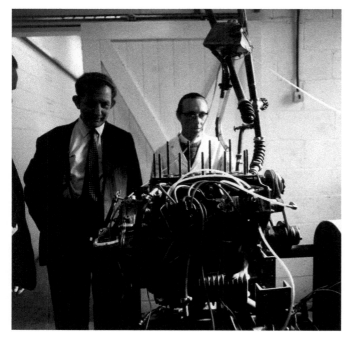

Daniel Richmond (left), the eccentric genius behind premiere Mini Cooper tuners Downton Engineering, studies an engine with Ray Sheppard on the test bed. (*MiniWorld* archive)

impressive list of tuning parts for the Mini Cooper S, allowing private owners to tune their cars almost to the specification of the then current works cars. The BMC works team always kept a few tricks up their sleeves though, as good works teams do.

The 1,275cc Mini Cooper S soldiered on in production a little longer than its smaller brother the Mini Cooper. A Mk3 version of the car was made with wind-up windows, internal door hinges and changes to colour and trim. However, British Leyland rid themselves of it too in 1971 by which time 45,147 Mini Cooper Ss of all types had been made. Given its success in competitions (which is the subject of chapter four), the Mini Cooper S created a golden halo around not only the Mini Cooper models but the entire Mini range. The halo of success still endures to this day and is regularly referenced as brand defining by BMW, the MINI's current manufacturers. Not bad for a model that went out of production fifty years ago!

An original-looking 1966 Morris Mini Cooper S pictured at a car show in Downton, Wiltshire. This particular car, finished in Tweed grey and Old English white, has the optional 4.5-inch J steel wheels and reclining front seats, as well as a vinyl sunroof. All were desirable optional extras in their day. (Peter Barker)

A beautiful Mk3 Mini Cooper S finished in British Leyland's startling orange colour. Undervalued compared to the earlier Mk1 and Mk2 Cooper S types, the Mk3 Mini Cooper S was the last contemporary Cooper product made under the original licensing agreement with BMC/BL. (Peter Barker)

Chapter 4
Mighty Mini – the Mini Cooper in Competition

As soon as the Mini Cooper was launched it hit the racetracks and rally stages of the world. This was, of course, exactly what it had been intended for and it was an instant success. Among the first competition drivers to appreciate the virtues of the Mini Cooper were two famous women: racing driver Christabel Carlisle and rally driver Pat Moss. As Christabel recalled:

> For 1962 I was given a Mini Cooper to race. The Cooper works team were supposed to finish first, second and third but I usually managed to divide them. I had learned a lot about slipstreaming from Mick Clare at Snetterton, so at Aintree in 1962 when the three works Coopers were in front I couldn't bear it. I managed to get very close to Tony Maggs and carefully count the laps. On the very last lap I slipstreamed his car up the back straight, pulling out to pass him on the inside of Melling Crossing. I was really relieved because it was no good for my reputation to be beaten by all three Cooper cars.

Don Moore leans into the Mini of Christabel Carlisle (centre of shot) to advise her on how to take a very wet race at Brands Hatch. Unphased by the much larger cars around her, Christabel gave the works Cooper boys a run for their money and brought some feminine charm to the race circuits of Britain. (*MiniWorld* archive)

Ann Wisdom (left) and Pat Moss (right) were one of Britain's best rally crews of the late 1950s and early 1960s. They were the first crew to rally a factory-prepared Mini Cooper, taking Morris Cooper 737ABL to overall wins on the Tulip Rally and German Rally in 1962. (*MiniWorld* archive)

While the new Mini Cooper was producing very close races on the circuits of Britain the rally world was also waking up to a new force in its midst. 'Stirling's Sister' and BMC factory team driver Pat Moss was an experienced rally driver with several major victories to her name. She was given a works Mini Cooper that was modified to rally specification for the 1962 Monte Carlo Rally.

> We really began to respect the Mini Cooper on that rally, but I still found it difficult to drive on the limit as it was so twitchy. With the Austin Healey 3000 or any other conventional car you had some warning of when it was about to leave the road. The Mini could understeer off so quickly that you had to have lightening reactions in order to catch it.

The understeer that Pat referred to was the tendency of a car to plough onwards in corners with the front wheels drifting across the road surface. With its front-wheel drive and front-mounted engine, the Mini Cooper tended to exhibit this behaviour until drivers learned to lift off the throttle mid corner, which brought the back round so they could regain control.

At the same time that the Mini Cooper was introduced another force entered the rally world, a twenty-seven-year-old ex-accountant and motoring journalist from Stafford named Stuart Turner. Stuart was appointed Competitions Manager of BMC in late 1961 just as the Mini Cooper was launched. With his no-nonsense but deep-thinking approach and a competitive streak that had caused him to be a winning rally navigator in his day, Stuart was exactly the right man to exploit the brilliant new car. First on his list of revolutionary ideas were drivers:

> I had no time for precious drivers. I wanted the best talent available and that was just starting to emerge from Scandinavia. I had sat alongside Erik Carlsson and won the 1960 RAC Rally so I knew just how good they were. It was around then that many top sportsmen and sportswomen were becoming professional for the first time and international rallying was no exception.

Stuart recruited two of the young men who would soon become synonymous with the Mini Cooper: Finnish drivers Rauno Aaltonen and Timo Makinen, collectively known as 'The Flying Finns'. They bought with them a whole new way of driving on the loose surfaced roads that were beginning to be the basis of rally stages, as Pat Moss recalled: 'The Scandinavians drove the Mini Cooper so that it was sideways on corners, thus preventing it going straight off.'

Rauno Aaltonen, however, saw the new Mini Cooper driving techniques as an extension of work he had already done with other models:

> Left foot braking (in which the brake pedal is operated with the driver's left foot while the right foot operates the throttle) has had a great deal written about it. I used it on SAABs and transferred it to the Mini Cooper. It is a technique that allows the driver to brake and steer at the same time but it is definitely for experts.

Above left: Stuart Turner (in glasses talking to BMC's Den Green) was the genius behind the rally success of the Mini Cooper. An accountant turned rally co-driver and journalist, Turner went on to mastermind the Escort's rally success for Ford during the 1970s. (McKlein)

Above right: Paddy Hopkirk (left), Timo Makinen (centre) and Rauno Aaltonen (right) don't look too downhearted having just been disqualified from the first three places in the 1966 Rallye Monte-Carlo. The headlamp dipping systems on their Mini Cooper S cars were declared illegal by the scrutineers of the Automobile Club of Monaco after the event. (*MiniWorld* archive)

In addition to the Flying Finns Stuart Turner also recruited a young Irishman with a talent for both driving and publicity: Paddy Hopkirk. The name of Paddy Hopkirk would later be permanently linked with that of the Mini Cooper but in the beginning, he was more interested in BMC's Austin Healey rally cars than the humble Mini Cooper:

> I remember being at Oulton Park race circuit and Stuart Turner turned up with one of the first Mini Cooper S types. I just fell in love with it there and then. The way it handled was so forgiving and after a short drive I was sure that this was the car for me.

Success on the racetracks came pretty soon for the Mini Cooper, with South African driver John Love winning the 1962 BRSCC National Saloon Car Championship in a Cooper Car Co. entered 997cc Mini Cooper. On the same team as John but forced to play second fiddle to him was the young racing baronet Sir John Whitmore.

> In that same year, 1962, we (the Cooper Car Co. team of three Mini Coopers) were entered in a race at Spa in Belgium. The local opposition didn't seem to be up to much and by the end of one lap we were several minutes ahead of any other car!

Overconfident, the Cooper boys tried to stage a dead heat for all three of their cars but were jumped by a locally driven DKW with 1 metre to go. So much for arrogance. With the coming of the Mini Cooper S, first in 1,071cc form and then in ultimate 1,275cc guise, the circuits of the world became the oyster of the horde of Mini Cooper racers. John Whitmore recalls:

> For 1963 we had the 1,071cc Cooper S engines and much bigger brakes. They were practically unbeatable. Halfway through the year John Cooper bought out the 1,275cc engine, which we tried in a six-hour relay race. It was simply amazing. I had

Cooper Car Co. works racing Mini Coopers in the paddock at Snetterton circuit during the 1962 season. John Love and John Whitmore drove similar cars to win the BRSCC National Saloon Car Championship in that year. (*MiniWorld* archive)

An Austin Cooper S leads the pack in a six-hour saloon car race. The 1,275cc Mini Cooper S was practically unbeatable in its first season of racing. (*MiniWorld* archive)

a ball with it! Coming out of corners in that car you could pass anything else on the racetrack. It was so much better than all the other cars at that time.

The two Johns, Love and Whitmore, were succeeded by two more Johns, Handley and Rhodes, as Cooper Car Co. team drivers. During the mid-1960s the Mini Cooper S seemed unbeatable among saloon cars on the racetrack, but a challenge was developing. In late 1967 Ford Europe announced the Escort and in 1968 it arrived at the races where it duly dominated. However, the Mini Cooper S still had a few breaths left as a top-flight race car as newcomer Gordon Spice explained:

In 1969 I was offered a drive with the newly formed Britax-Cooper-Downton team in the British Saloon Car Championship. Steve Neal and I had an eight-port fuel injected

Steve Neal (left) and Gordon Spice (right) were the fortunate drivers of the Britax-Cooper-Downton Mini Cooper S racing cars during the 1969 season. (Gordon Spice)

Gordon Spice looks confident in his Britax-Cooper-Downton racing Mini Cooper S from 1969. Beautifully prepared in striking yellow and black, the B-C-D cars of Gordon Spice and fellow driver Steve Neal gave the Ford Escort of Chris Craft a run for its money but could not win. (Gordon Spice)

race Mini Cooper S, each with 12-inch wheels, a limited slip differential and finished in bright yellow and black. They put out 130 bhp each and were pretty physical to drive. After a season's racing we beat our Mini mounted rivals in the Abingdon (BL Competitions Department) team but had to give best in the Championship's 1,300cc class to Chris Craft in his Broadspeed Escort. I finished second.

While the meticulously prepared Mini Cooper S race cars were cleaning up on the track, the rally stage too was being dominated by this tiny battle box. With the announcement of the 1,071cc Mini Cooper S in 1963, a new era of rally domination was opening up for BMC's Competitions Department. Rauno Aaltonen and his regular co-driver Tony Ambrose took a very early Mini Cooper S on the 1963 Alpine Rally in June of that year and won the

Gordon Spice in the Mini Cooper S leads Chris Craft in the Ford Escort at Mallory Park in 1969. The racing Mini Cooper S was at the final stage of its factory sponsored development in this year and gave 130 bhp from a 1,300cc fuel-injected engine. (Gordon Spice)

Touring Car category. It was Paddy Hopkirk who really lit a torch for the Mini Cooper S and its manufacturers with a class win and third overall in the Tour de France Automobile that September. As Paddy recalled,

> George Harriman, the Chairman of BMC, was at the London Motorshow in October '63 and was impressed with the number of orders for Mini Cooper S types coming in from the French dealers. Each one was asking for 100 cars. 'What have you been doing over there?' he asked me. So I explained all about the Tour de France. I don't think he'd ever made a direct connection between motorsport success and sales success before.

Paddy's star was to climb even higher on his next Continental event in the very same Mini Cooper S, registered 33EJB, that he had driven in the Tour de France. The event did not start well for the Mini Cooper S crew, however:

> Navigator Henry Liddon and I were sent to start the 1964 Monte Carlo Rally from Minsk in Russia. BMC exported no cars to Russia so we were there to fly the flag a little. It was so cold at night that the Mini froze solid. Door locks, windows and the engine oil just froze up in the temperature of minus 40 degrees centigrade. We had to tow the car round and round the main square to warm it up before we could start it. This drew derision from the Russian competitors who said 'Our cars are superior. They have electric starters and don't need to be towed to start them!'

Once away from Minsk, Paddy and Henry travelled through Poland, Czechoslovakia, Germany and the Netherlands before reaching the concentration point in France. There were still problems to overcome, however:

Rauno Aaltonen with Tony Ambrose in the very first works rally Mini Cooper S, 277EBL, pulling away from a service point during the 1963 Alpine Rally. They won the Touring category of the event, the first international success for this brand new 1,071cc model. (Mini Cooper Register)

We were travelling through Colmars when Henry told me to take a right fork. I shot up this road only to find a policeman at the end of it. I had gone the wrong way up a one-way street. He stopped us and asked for our road book in order to penalise us for a traffic violation. (This would certainly have lost them the rally). Henry, being an English gentleman, was about to give him the book when I hurriedly told him to hide it. I then gave the policeman a story about how I'd retired from the rally as my mother had died and I was on my way home to her funeral. He was most sympathetic and let us go on our way. I would have loved to have seen his face when he read in the paper a few days later that we'd actually gone on to win the rally.

Ford of America had announced that they were going to win the Monte Carlo Rally in 1964 and had sent over a formidable team of very special lightweight Ford Falcons to be driven by top European drivers. One of their team, Bo Ljungfeld, was leading the rally on scratch and it seemed that Ford had the event all sewn up.

Bo Lungfeld, in one of the Ford Falcons, was actually much quicker than us on almost every stage. However, a handicap was applied to allow cars of all sizes to compete equally and it was this that gave us the edge. On the way down the Col de Turini I was stopped by Competitions Manager Stuart Turner who asked how we'd done. I replied that we'd done all we could do. We'd made no mistakes anywhere. I was asleep in my hotel when Bernard Cahier, a journalist, called me at 4.30 a.m. to say that he'd seen the provisional calculations and that provided that if I did nothing wrong on the final grand prix circuit test we would win. I could hardly believe it and with my heart in my mouth completed the circuit next morning with something like 50 seconds in hand to win the 33rd Monte Carlo Rally.

Paddy Hopkirk and Henry Liddon scoot their Mini Cooper S over the packed snow of the Col de Turini to win the 1964 Rallye Monte-Carlo. 33EJB was retired to become an icon following this famous win and is today reputedly the most valuable Mini Cooper on earth. (McKlein)

Broadcaster and BMC's Director of Publicity Raymond Baxter finds his works Austin Cooper with its wheels neatly removed by some prankster after the 1964 Rallye Monte-Carlo. BMC organised a substantial party in Monte Carlo following Paddy Hopkirk's win and more than a few practical jokes were played. (*MiniWorld* archive)

Paddy Hopkirk (sitting on the car) and Henry Liddon with their 1964 Rallye Monte-Carlo-winning Morris Cooper S 33EJB at Lydd Airport. Henry Liddon navigated two drivers to Monte Carlo wins in Mini Coopers, Paddy Hopkirk in 1964 and Rauno Aaltonen in 1967. (*MiniWorld* archive)

Paddy Hopkirk and Henry Liddon descend the stairs of their Caravelle on their return to London from a famous Monte Carlo victory. (*MiniWorld* archive)

Nothing succeeds like success and this win catapulted Paddy Hopkirk and the Mini Cooper S into permanent stardom. The spectre of this tiny 1,100cc car beating the mighty Ford Falcons at Monte Carlo turned the Mini Cooper S from a sporting gamble by BMC into a most desirable item. Suddenly it was cooler to be seen in a Mini Cooper S than a Rolls-Royce, Bentley or Mercedes. By the end of 1964 over 7,300 Mini Cooper S types had been made in Britain of which more than 40 per cent were exported. This was exactly the kind of foreign currency earnings that BMC needed and what's more the Mini Cooper S was raising Britain's standing all round the world. It was, as Mr Bridger, a central character of the 1969 film *The Italian Job*, would later say, 'a matter of prestige'.

BMC's Competitions Department swiftly capitalised on their victory. Another two outright wins followed for the Mini Cooper S in the Tulip Rally and the Austrian Alpine Rally, as well as several class wins during 1964. Despite crashing out of November's RAC Rally Paddy Hopkirk and his colleagues were ready for another attack on the Monte Carlo Rally in early 1965. Could a Mini really win again? Garage proprietor Paul Easter from Stony Stratford in Buckinghamshire was invited to co-drive for Finnish star Timo Makinen on the event. Clearly BMC were out to win again, as he recalled:

Timo was entered in Group 3, the GT (modified) category, in a 1,275cc Mini Cooper S registered AJB 44B. We went out to the Alps in December and practiced the stages for six weeks before the event. We started from Stockholm (running at No. 52). We were the first car to arrive in Gap and the controller entered our arrival time on the time card, not realising that we were early (weather conditions were so bad). Timo was just fantastic, a genius at work. In blizzard conditions he kept the car on the road even though the snow came over the Mini's roof at times, and he drove at such speed that we did not lose any time at all on the way to Monte – the only car to do so. After Gap we were running first on the road; we had passed all 51 cars ahead of us! Thirty-five of the original 239 cars got to Monte Carlo and of those 35 only 22 completed the Mountain Circuit (the final stages).

A speeding Timo Makinen with Paul Easter pass the Ranch Bar at the top of the Col de Turini to win the 1965 Rallye Monte-Carlo. Their winning margin was nineteen minutes and fifty-seven seconds, a crushing victory in this epically snowy event. (McKlein)

A trio of works Mini Cooper Ss presented for scrutineering at the start of the 1965 Alpine Rally. The drivers are, from front to rear, Paddy Hopkirk, Pauline Mayman and Timo Makinen. Note the externally mounted air horns on the front bumper to warn of the car's speedy arrival. (Mini Cooper Register)

Timo Makinen recalled this epic drive in an interview with the author in 2004:

> To my delight I was teamed up with Paul Easter for the 1965 Rallye Monte-Carlo in a works Mini Cooper S. We chose to start from Stockholm as it was better to run on properly ploughed roads in bad weather and in Scandinavia they know how to keep the roads open. We had the longest run into Monte Carlo, four nights on the road. The journey from Chambery to Monte Carlo was just fantastic with deep dry snow, over the roof of the Mini sometimes, but we had the best car and the best tyres for the conditions. I also had the will to win, I was really determined. We passed 20 or 30 cars, some of them well off the road. We were so early at some of the controls that we had time for a drink in a bar!

This was a simply amazing victory for Timo Makinen, Paul Easter, BMC and the Mini Cooper S. Although it grabbed the contemporary headlines a little less than the 1964 result, for those 'in the know' it was a more impressive win. There was no handicap needed to give the Mini Cooper S an edge in 1965. Makinen and Easter annihilated the opposition, winning by nearly twenty minutes, which consigned German driver Eugen Bohringer in a Porsche to second place and former Mini Cooper driver Pat Moss, now in a SAAB, to third. Only these two cars finished within thirty minutes of the winning Mini Cooper S – the rest of the field was even further behind. Wild celebrations ensued at a smart restaurant in Monte Carlo during which BMC Competitions Department supervisor Doug Watts was seen riding a donkey between the tables and Mini designer Alec Issigonis was spotted 'balancing on the floodlit rocks beside the restaurant, swaying to the music' according to Assistant Competitions Manager Bill Price.

During 1965 factory-entered BMC Mini Cooper S cars won no less than seven further international European rallies and Rauno Aaltonen became European Rally Champion. A towering achievement for the works Mini Cooper S and its supremely talented crews backed by the best factory Competitions Department in the world at that time. At this point the BMC operation was at its peak. However, during that year the first suggestions of a forthcoming downfall began to be heard. Outstanding Swedish rally driver and ambassador for SAAB cars Erik Carlsson told me in 2003: 'I warned the BMC team that they were becoming too confident. They thought that they could do anything. People were becoming resentful of their success and this would lead to trouble.'

These were prescient words indeed. During 1965 the FIA (Fédération Internationale de l'Automobile), governing body of world motorsport, issued a new version of the regulations covering cars entered in rallies. This document, known as Appendix J, defined a new 'showroom class' of rally car Group 1 in Category A. Qualification for this class demanded that 5,000 identical vehicles to the one entered should have been made within a year. This was a substantial number, unlikely to be met by a car made simply for competition use. When the regulations for the 1966 Monte Carlo Rally appeared in October 1965 it was immediately clear to Stuart Turner and others that only a Group 1 car stood any chance of success. More highly tuned formulae such as Groups 2 or 3 in which the Mini Cooper S had previously been entered would be handicapped in such a way that victory for these cars was impossible. Writing in mid-1965, Stuart Turner observed:

It is possible that with the advent of the 1966 Appendix J some rallies will include the new Group 1 of Category A. The modifications allowed in this Group are few. Lights may be changed provided they remain legal, but only two additional lights may be added.

This last phrase was to haunt BMC not long after. At the same time as these regulations were being revised quartz-iodine headlamp bulbs were being developed for cars. These new bulbs produced a high intensity white light and far outperformed the old tungsten filament bulbs previously available. BMC, along with other competitive manufacturers, naturally sourced such bulbs and fitted them to their rally cars for the 1966 Monte Carlo Rally, as Bill Price BMC Deputy Competitions Manager recalled:

> We prepared a new allocation of Cooper Ss for our drivers and incorporated the new quartz iodine headlamp bulbs which had just been developed. At that stage in their development these new prototype bulbs carried only a single filament due to the very high temperatures at which they ran, and so dipping to a second filament within the headlamp in the usual way was not possible.

Also according to Bill Price, BMC Competitions Department staff utilised an unusual method of dipping these single filament bulbs in order to not blind oncoming traffic at night and to comply with highway regulations.

> Lucas had done some work with the Lancashire Police force on a 'dim-dip' system using a resistance to dim the headlamps. They had tested this system and believed it to comply with both British and European traffic regulations. During the recces (reconnaissance journeys along the rally route) crews took cars with these new lighting systems out with them to test and although the results were very positive there were some reports that local police had not liked the new lighting arrangements.

Service for the Mini Cooper S of Rauno Aaltonen and Tony Ambrose during the 1966 Rallye Monte-Carlo. Disqualification from second place on a lighting technicality awaited this highly professional and successful rally crew. (Mini Cooper Register)

Determined concentration on the faces of Timo Makinen and Paul Easter as they race towards another victory in the 1966 Rallye Monte-Carlo. Their Group 1 showroom class Mini Cooper S was disqualified for the illegality of its headlamp dipping system. (McKlein)

Roadside service for the Mini Cooper S of Timo Makinen (right) and Paul Easter (centre) during the 1966 Rallye Monte-Carlo. Spare tyres and fuel were carried inside and on the rally cars during the initial run into Monte Carlo. (Mini Cooper Register)

Once the rally had started it swiftly became clear that British cars and in particular BMC's Mini Cooper S models were going to win the 1966 Monte Carlo Rally. On their arrival in Monaco the three works Minis were in first, second and third positions and in line for the Manufacturer's Team Award – absolute domination for the third year running. This time the Automobile Club of Monaco (ACM) were not going to let such a thing happen, particularly not in the 100th year of the Principality of Monaco, which had been founded in 1866. How could it be that cars in standard showroom condition could annihilate all other opposition like this? Rumours began circulating that BMC must have swapped cars for much more highly tuned versions during the rally – this was untrue. Then the three works Minis were taken from the finish line to a garage in Monaco where mechanics stripped them for nearly eighteen hours trying to find discrepancies with the standard specification of the cars; they found nothing. Finally President of the ACM Louis Chiron announced the results of the rally and the three works Mini Cooper S types plus the works Lotus Cortina of British driver Roger Clark and the factory-entered Hillman Imp of Irish driver Rosemary Smith, who had won the Ladies Prize, were all missing from the list. They had been disqualified as their lighting systems were deemed not to have been in accordance with FIA Appendix J. This was the flimsiest of excuses for excluding all five winning cars from Britain. Elevated to winner was Finnish driver Pauli Toivonen, whose works Citroen DS21 had arrived at the finish line with standard headlamp bulbs fitted. Toivonen was reputedly disgusted at the treatment of his fellow Finns Makinen and Aaltonen, who had been disqualified from first and second places respectively and refused to drive for Citroen ever again.

Immediately protests were made firstly to the ACM, who rejected them, and subsequently to the FIA through the RAC back in Britain. These too were rejected and to this day the winner of the 1966 Monte Carlo Rally is listed as Pauli Toivonen driving a Citroen. BMC, however, still put on a massive party, this time back in London where the three disqualified Mini Coopers were celebrated in the press and on TV just as though they had won the rally. As Bill Price put it: 'Greater publicity was achieved for BMC by the disqualification than if we had actually won the rally!'

After this fiasco it took some time for the Automobile Club of Monaco to regain the respect in which they had once been held in Britain. BMC and the Mini Cooper S, however, carried on their winning ways. Wins on eight international rallies (including three for Tony Fall, a young car salesman from Bradford in Yorkshire who was newly recruited to the team) were supported by a host of other successes. While the opposition in the shape of Porsche, Ford and Lancia were starting to eat into the Mini's domination, the BMC team had a good year in 1966 despite its inglorious start.

1967 was the watershed year for BMC. Rauno Aaltonen was the only one of BMC's 'big three' drivers not to have won the Monte Carlo Rally and he was burning to win that year, as he remembered:

On the 1966 Monte Timo had been half a minute faster than me on the Col de Granier stage. I was determined that this would not happen in the 1967 event so I spent two weeks practicing this stage alone. On the rally I was two minutes faster over this stage than the next car and the organisers thought there was a mistake with the timing and altered my time card so that I was only a few seconds faster. I was very angry and drove even faster so by the start of the last stage, the Turini stage, I was 15 seconds ahead of the second placed car, which was a Porsche.

Tony Fall and Mike Wood with their works Mini Cooper S await scrutineering and signing on for the 1966 Alpine Rally in Marseille. Tony winning an Alpine Cup in the previous year's event helped him to get a full works drive for 1966. (Mini Cooper Register)

Rauno Aaltonen shuts the door of his works Morris Cooper S LBL6D during the 1967 Rallye Monte-Carlo, which he won with Henry Liddon. A wealth of special and highly desirable equipment is on display in this beautifully prepared car, which now resides in the British Motor Museum at Gaydon. (Mini Cooper Register)

37

A famous photograph of Rauno Aaltonen and Henry Liddon hard at work in the Morris Cooper S on their way to winning the 1967 Rallye Monte-Carlo. The rally was won by the smallest of margins after a miraculous drive over the final stage, the Col de Turini, in falling snow. (Mini Cooper Register)

A boulder mysteriously fell into the road in front of the Morris Cooper S of Timo Makinen and Paul Easter during the final night of the 1967 Rallye Monte-Carlo. It smashed the front-mounted oil cooler, putting the front running crew out of the rally. (Mini Cooper Register)

Paddy Hopkirk displays a perfect drift angle descending the Col de Turini on snow in the Austin Cooper S he shared with Ron Crellin during the 1967 Rallye Monte-Carlo. They finished sixth overall as they were hampered by an inappropriate tyre choice. (Mini Cooper Register)

Paddy Hopkirk, with Ron Crellin, has a quick word with spectators through the window of their works Austin Cooper S LBL 666D during the 1967 Rallye Monte-Carlo. (Mini Cooper Register)

The ACM had announced that for 1967 cars in Category 1 could use only eight tyres on the competitive sections of the rally. Category 2 cars could use an unlimited number of tyres but would have to accept a 12 per cent handicap, which would make them effectively uncompetitive. BMC and other factory teams entered their drivers in Category 1 and left it to each driver to make their choice of tyres. Rauno decided to go one step further and took a set of tyres into his hotel room on the night before the final section then sat up most of the night with a compressor and stud gun grading the protrusion of the studs across the tyre. This demon trick gave him a slight advantage in terms of tyre wear and when he was lining up for that final stage his tyres had a little more life left in them than those of the opposition. So the stage was set for what can only be described as a Mini miracle. Again in the words of Rauno Aaltonen:

The Porsche did its run on dry tarmac and then there was an accident on the stage just as I was about to start (a spectator's car had fallen onto the stage!) An ambulance was called and I had to switch the engine off and wait. While I was waiting snow started to fall and by the time I started my run it was thick on the road. When I got to the summit my co-driver Henry Liddon told me I was 3 minutes down on my practice time for the stage. I gave it everything; I took all the bends flat in fourth gear going downhill. All was fine until I felt the car sliding on ice under the snow. We shot off the road and I remember seeing the headlights shine on the trees. We fell onto the side of the mountain and I managed to steer between the snow-clad boulders as we sped downhill. The car jumped a snowbank and landed back on the road a few hundred metres below where we had left it. We were facing the wrong way so I handbraked the car round and raced to the end of the stage, winning the rally by 13 seconds. We kept very quiet about this at the time as taking a shortcut on a stage even by mistake was illegal.

The crew of the works Lancia who had been beaten into second place by this extraordinary event were not best pleased and were mystified as to how Aaltonen and Liddon had pulled in front of them. They had to accept the result, however, and so the Mini Cooper S in the hands of BMC's Competition Department and its talented crews won the world's most famous rally for the third time.

Five further international rally wins were recorded by BMC's team using the Mini Cooper S during 1967. Possibly the most impressive of these was the victory of Paddy Hopkirk, co-driven by Ron Crellin, in the Alpine Rally of that year. Aided by Timo Makinen, who drove his highly tuned Group 6 Mini Cooper S into the ground as pacemaker for the rally, Hopkirk kept his cool and conserved his similar car just long enough to see the opposition break up in a desperate battle for the lead. It is said that the French Alpine Rally of 1967 was the fastest event ever promoted on open roads and for a Mini to win it was simply miraculous. As things turned out this was the final major international rally win for the works Mini Cooper S. The rally year ended with last minute cancellation of the RAC Rally of Great Britain due to a widespread outbreak of foot and mouth disease in the countryside. This left manufacturers with some highly tuned machinery including BMC, who had managed to shoehorn Lucas mechanical fuel injection under the bonnet of a Mini Cooper S entered in Group 6 for Timo Makinen. The rally was replaced by a televised special stage at Camberley in Surrey, which at least gave TV viewers something to watch.

Prize-giving in the courtyard of the Palace at Monaco. Rauno Aaltonen (in the dark suit behind the car) and Henry Liddon (with his back to the camera) look on as their winning Morris Cooper S is piled high with cups and trophies. 1967 Rallye Monte-Carlo. (*MiniWorld* archive)

Rauno Aaltonen (left) and Henry Liddon (right) with works Morris Mini Cooper S LBL 6D arrive back in Britain at Lydd Airport having just won the 1967 Rallye Monte-Carlo. This was the last of the Mini Cooper's three wins at Monte Carlo, a wonderful record for such a small car. (*MiniWorld* archive)

Co-driver Paul Easter seems to be aiming a kick at the lightweight Group 6 Mini Cooper S he shared with Timo Makinen during the 1967 Alpine Rally, shown here at a halt in Alpe d'Huez. (*MiniWorld* archive)

Paddy Hopkirk and Ron Crellin scream up a Col in their lightweight Group 6 works Mini Cooper S to win the 1967 Alpine Rally. This event was reputedly the fastest rally using open public roads ever promoted in Europe. (Mini Cooper Register)

Right: The emblem of the Association Sportive within the Automobile Club de Marseille et Provence, organisers of the fearsome French Alpine Rally between 1932 and 1971. (ACMP)

Below: Timo Makinen and Tony Fall blast over a televised special stage in the Group 6 fuel-injected Mini Cooper S. Cancellation of the 1967 RAC Rally due to an outbreak of bovine foot and mouth disease left BMC with some unused and powerful rally machinery. (McKlein)

1968 proved to be a year too far for the works Mini Cooper S in rallying. Porsche had finally got the 911 'sorted' for international rally use and in a year with no snow on the Monte Carlo Rally they used their car's power to win, finishing in first and second places. The works Mini Cooper S cars were third, fourth and fifth in their swansong at Monte Carlo. This was not achieved without drama however, as their prototype split-Weber carburetors came under suspicion from the same scrutineer who had caused the demise of the factory Mini Cooper Ss in 1966. This time, however, reason prevailed and the Minis kept their high, if not winning, places. No further international victories were recorded and as on the racetrack the Mini Cooper S was overtaken by newer, faster models on the rally stages of the world. Valiant attempts were made to achieve one last victory by various rally crews including Paddy Hopkirk and Irish co-driver Terry Harryman, who finished second in the 1969 Circuit of Ireland Rally with their lightweight Group 6 Mini Cooper S, after a furious battle with Roger Clark in a Ford Escort Twin Cam. The Ford Escort swiftly replaced the Mini Cooper S as the car of choice in British rallying at all levels and the Mini Cooper's rally bubble was burst.

The Mini Cooper and Cooper S succeeded spectacularly at all levels of motorsport just as their creators had intended. Although the top-level career of these cars was now over the aura of success generated by the Mini Cooper saw it through some very lean times until an unexpected rebirth.

Old Mini Cooper S rally cars being used for reconnaissance prior to the 1968 Monte Carlo Rally. Professional crews spent weeks surveying the route and practising before a major event such as this. (Mini Cooper Register)

A works Mini Cooper S at speed in practice for the 1968 Monte Carlo Rally. Relentless rehearsal for the rally by the BMC team helped give them the edge over their rivals on several occasions but not on this one as they were beaten by Porsche. (Mini Cooper Register)

Crowded service point for the works Mini Cooper S of Tony Fall and Mike Wood during the 1968 Monte Carlo Rally. Technicians from brake supplier Ferodo can be seen working at the rear of the car while BMC mechanics work at the front. (Mini Cooper Register)

Chapter 5

'Demise and Rebirth': The End of the Original Mini Cooper and Dawn of a New Era

While the Mini Cooper S had been basking in the limelight of motorsport victory, stagnation, corruption and decay had been eating away at the British motor industry. As the largest motor manufacturer in Britain this was particularly evident at BMC. Years of inept management, poor accounting, internal rivalries, a reluctance to invest or modernise and increasingly militant trade unions all contributed to the demise of the British motor industry. BMC, now in distress, was absorbed into British Leyland along with formerly proud independent Coventry-based motor companies Jaguar Cars and Standard-Triumph Ltd. in May 1968. The resulting corporation was overseen by Donald Stokes, a former truck and bus salesman who underestimated the challenge of uniting the major part of the British motor industry into one company. He closed the world-famous British Leyland Competitions Department following their failure (as he saw it) to win the 1970 World Cup Rally from Ford. In fact Brian Culcheth came a fine second overall in a Competitions Department prepared Triumph 2.5Pi but that wasn't good enough to save the department.

As far as the Mini Cooper was concerned the agreement with John Cooper was terminated as soon as it could decently be arranged (during 1971, which was the tenth anniversary of the Mini Cooper's introduction). This was done on the grounds that the use of Cooper's name was expensive and was pushing up insurance premiums for ordinary motorists who wanted to drive a hot Mini. In place of the now defunct Mini Cooper S British Leyland had the temerity to introduce the lukewarm Mini Clubman based 1275GT. With a downgraded engine specification, Dunlop Denovo 'run-flat' tyres and Ford-style body graphics, this was a Mini in denial. The 1275GT simply didn't cut it compared to the old Cooper S despite the fact that it had an engine capacity of the same volume (1,275cc). It didn't have the same get up and go as the Mini Cooper S and none of its hard-earned glamour.

As the dismal 1970s wore on in Britain another oil crisis loomed, this time due to tensions between Israel and the Arab world. As a consequence in 1975 the humble Mini (in either 850cc or more usually 1,000cc guise) briefly became Britain's bestselling car. An attempt by British Leyland, now BL, to replace the Mini also came and went and although the Austin Mini-Metro went on sale in 1979, the Mini soldiered on still with its 998cc engine throughout the next decade. It seemed that the Mini would never die, but somehow it was the walking dead: a model that Rover Group, as the manufacturer was by now called, would not invest in but at the same time could not kill. All of a sudden, however, another of those miracles upon which the Mini seems to have thrived suddenly occurred.

The unfortunate Mini Clubman and 1275GT were supposed to follow on where the Mini Cooper and Cooper S left off in 1970/71. It didn't work and the new square-nosed cars were themselves deleted after ten years' production. (Peter Barker)

In 1989 the recently introduced chairman of Rover, Canadian lawyer Graham Day, announced that the company were going to offer John Cooper Garages (John Cooper's current business venture) conversions on 998cc Minis sold as new and that the manufacturer's warranty would be honoured on these cars by dealers. At the same time two new versions of the Mini were introduced in either a flame red body colour with a white roof or a British racing green body colour, also with a white roof. This was the 998cc Mini Cooper reborn! As a young householder with my first salaried job I rushed round to my local Rover dealership, put down a deposit and ordered one of these cars. After what seemed an interminable (actually six weeks) wait the car was delivered, taken to John Cooper Garages in Ferring and converted to Cooper specification. It was a revelation. Spirited performance (limited only by the mechanical fuel pump, which simply could not deliver enough fuel to keep up with the tuned car's consumption) allied to fantastic handling made the new Mini Cooper a dream to drive. By now riding on 12-inch wheels rather than the 10-inch wheels of the 1960s models this new Cooperised Mini had adequate disc brakes and actually stopped when the driver required. Twin 1.25-inch SU carburettors, a Janspeed modified cylinder head and free-flowing exhaust echoed 1960s practice but brought it up to date as the new Mini Cooper used unleaded fuel at a very reasonable rate if driven moderately (which it almost never was). Suddenly the Mini Cooper was back in business.

Chapter 6
'Rover's Return' – the Rebirth of the Mini Cooper

Emboldened by a resurgence of interest in the Mini, which coincided with its thirtieth anniversary in 1989, and by the popularity of John Cooper's tuning kits for the 1,000cc Mini, Rover took the plunge and once again introduced the Mini Cooper to series production in July 1990. This was an unprecedented move within the British motor industry. Never in recorded history had a major manufacturer discontinued a model only to revive it twenty years later. Full marks must go to Rover's management for its bravery and to Rover Special Products or RSP, the division which developed the car, for its relaunch in a remarkably short time.

In cooperation with the ever-enthusiastic John Cooper a specification that included a 1,275cc single carburetor engine, 'Minilite'-style 12-inch alloy wheels and slightly more luxurious interior trim was developed. A batch of 1,000 Mini Coopers was made for the UK, with another 650 especially made for Japan, which had become the Mini's biggest export market. This first batch, developed and produced by RSP, sold out immediately, prompting Rover to introduce a mainstream version in 1991, thirty years after the introduction of the first Austin and Morris Mini Coopers. This mainstream Rover Cooper (as it came to be known) had a similar mechanical specification to the RSP cars but was slightly less lavish in its interior trim and exterior decoration. Sales were buoyant and suddenly the Mini Cooper was looking as fresh and relevant as it had been in 1961. Alastair Vines, an engineer at Rover's New Model Centre, who were instrumental in the launch of the Rover Cooper, remembers the speedy development of this new model:

> I remember a meeting at Rover's plant at Fletchampstead North in Coventry in late 1989. John Cooper was there, as was chief stylist Geoff Upex and other senior staff. The go ahead had been given to put the Mini Cooper back into volume production and we were tasked with producing prototypes by April 1990. We achieved this and got the Rover Cooper into volume production, although there were some difficulties with supplies of both the special exhaust system and the temperature sender that operated the electric cooling fan.

To keep up with emissions regulations, the following year Rover introduced single point fuel injection to the Mini Cooper for the 1993 model year. This did little for performance but it did mean that the Mini could stay in production during the mid-1990s, which it could not have done using a carburetor as it would no longer have met European emissions regulations. As the 1990s wore on continued tightening of emissions regulations became a serious problem for the Mini Cooper with its 1950s derived A series engine. To keep the car in production up to the turn of the century, at which point new owners of Rover, BMW, intended to replace the Mini, a whole new multipoint fuel injection system (or MPi for short) was designed and developed by Rover engineers. Foremost among these engineers was a young man called Mike Theaker. Mike recalled the difficulties associated with developing multipoint fuel injection for an engine as old as the Mini Cooper's:

Some people said it couldn't be done but I was sure it was possible. After many hours of detailed calculations and against the wishes of some of Rover's senior management I decided to modify one of our development cars. Working undercover at Gaydon (Rover's design and development facility in Warwickshire, England) we built a prototype that fired and ran at the first touch of the key. The essential problem was that the Mini cylinder head has 'siamesed' ports. That is one inlet port feeds two cylinders – which need fuel pulses at different times in the engine's cycle. We developed a new principal called 'bi-directional pulsewidth stretching', which was the subject of a patent granted in my name in 1995. The combination of BMW's will and John Cooper's insistence meant that productionising of the system took place and it was introduced in 1996.

Even in the last few years of its second production life the Issigonis/Cooper-inspired Mini Cooper was still breaking new ground and delighting owners who continued to buy it in enough quantity that it remained on sale throughout a fourth decade.

With the classic Mini's replacement, the MINI, under development by BMW from the mid-1990s the end had to come for the little car. On Wednesday 4 October 2000 the fateful moment came when the last classic Mini made, a red and silver Mini Cooper, rolled off the production line at Longbridge. Geoff Powell, production manager on the Mini line, recalled that final day:

We had 250 press people at the ceremony and all those who had worked on the Mini line for 10 years or more walked behind the last car as it was driven off the end of the production line. Celebrity guest Lulu was a bit nervous about driving the car over the 'dogs' (retaining pins) that held it to the line and so I offered to do it for her. She sat in the passenger seat while I drove and that's how the last Mini left the production line.

British racing green and silver colour the body of this last edition Mini Cooper 500. Among the final Mini Coopers to be manufactured using the Issigonis design, these cars were carefully built by a dedicated workforce who were well aware that the new MINI Cooper was just over the horizon. (Peter Barker)

Above: Interior of a 1999 Mini Cooper 500. A limited edition, these final cars had a special interior treatment but no more power than the standard Mini Cooper. (Peter Barker)

Right: Little pack of goodies given away with the Mini Cooper 500. They are collectable items now. (Peter Barker)

More than 5 million classic Minis of all types were made between 1959 and 2000 and a good percentage of those were Mini Coopers. As the last classic Mini Cooper drove away from Longbridge, its tiny transfer gears whining, onlookers could have been forgiven for thinking that this was not the end of an era and that all affection would move seamlessly onto the new MINI Cooper, which was just commencing production on the site of the old Morris factory at Cowley in Oxford. Life is rarely that straightforward, however.

Chapter 7
An Enduring Legacy: Mini Cooper in the Twenty-first Century

In early 2002 I took a brand new MINI Cooper, one of the first delivered, to visit Mini suspension designer Dr Alex Moulton at his home in Wiltshire, England. This was the first time that he had had a chance to ride in and evaluate the new car that bore both the names of his finest automotive creation and that of his friend John Cooper (who had died in 2000). After a short ride on the roads around his home and in the company of American suspension engineer Doug Milliken, who also happened to be there, Alex pronounced his verdict.

It's enormous. The original Mini was the best packaged car of all time – this is an example of how not to do it. The interior space is not much bigger than the old Mini, but it's huge on the outside. The crash protection has been taken too far. I mean what do you want, an armoured car?

The author talks with Jurgen Hedrich, director of MINI Plant Oxford, at the Family Day in 2010. By this time enmity between new MINI owners BMW and owners of the older Mini models had died away and MINI Plant Oxford staff willingly assisted Mini entries for the Rallye Monte-Carlo Historique in subsequent years. (Helen Hargest)

He also declared that the suspension was 'too stiff and gave a most uncomfortable ride'. Clearly there was not much sympathy there for the new BMW designed and developed successor to the Mini Cooper.

Alex Moulton's view was extreme but it was echoed in a smaller way among many Mini Cooper enthusiasts at the time, particularly in the UK. The MINI Cooper was seen as a German imposition upon a British brand and some fairly hostile behaviour between owners of new and old models was reported. BMW's agents in the UK did not help the new car's case by ruthlessly pursuing anyone who traded on the name 'Mini', which was now a trademark of BMW AG.

As time went by and sales of the MINI Cooper took off tensions eased and the new car became accepted. Today, twenty years later and with many varieties of the MINI Cooper and Cooper S a familiar sight on our roads, it is hard to imagine that there was ever a problem. Intelligent and inclusive marketing by BMW, as well as the passage of time, have done the trick and looking back now the continuation from Mini Cooper to MINI Cooper seems obvious. Whatever your point of view it is satisfying that the names MINI and Cooper are still associated in a product that continues to sell and give pleasure to its owners and drivers.

A proud moment: former works Mini Cooper driver Paddy Hopkirk holds the Coupe des Alpes (Alpine Cup) awarded to the author and Willy Cave for winning the 2010 Rallye des Alpes Historique in this 1965 Mini Cooper S. Interestingly Willy Cave was also Paddy Hopkirk's navigator in a Triumph TR3 during the 1956 Alpine Rally. (Helen Hargest)

Chapter 8
The Mini Cooper in Popular Culture

As the Mini Cooper phenomenon developed so did references to it in popular culture, particularly in films and on TV. Initially the Mini Cooper was a bit part actor in 1960s TV shows and films but without a starring role. That is until 1966/67 when the BBC, in a bid to counter the highly successful ITV series *The Avengers*, launched *Adam Adamant Lives!* In what might now be termed a mini-series (no pun intended) the main character, played by Gerald Harper, an Edwardian adventurer named Adam Adamant who has somehow hibernated for 100 years, wakes up to find himself in 1967. Over two series and twenty-nine episodes, Adam comes to terms with life in London during the 1960s while driving a very special brown and gold coloured Mini Cooper S registered AA1 000. This car, extensively modified by coachbuilders Harold Radford, who were better known at the time for their limousine conversions, was exactly the right town conveyance for an Edwardian man of action. It starred in its own right alongside Gerald Harper in much the same way that Emma Peel's Lotus Elan or John Steed's vintage Bentley did in the rival show *The Avengers*. Despite their efforts the BBC programme could not approach the cult status of *The Avengers* and no further series were made.

This year-long burst of stardom for the Mini Cooper was nothing compared to what was coming next. At around the same time that *Adam Adamant Lives!* was being broadcast a young and frustrated British TV writer named Troy Kennedy Martin was trying to break into films. Using the idea of a big bank heist in Italy and a deliberately manipulated computerised traffic jam during the robbery (mainframe computers were cutting edge technology in the 1960s), Kennedy Martin came up with a cheeky script he called *The Italian Job*.

Although he didn't know it at the time Troy Kennedy Martin contributed to the future immortality of the script's leading character, played by Michael Caine (to whom he showed the script with immediately positive results), as well as a trio of red, white and blue Mini Cooper Ss. With the backing of Michael Caine the film was commissioned by Paramount Pictures in 1969 and produced by Michael Deeley. Peter Collinson was recruited as director and in addition to Michael Caine the cast included the unlikely combination of comedian Benny Hill and English stage actor and sophisticate Noel Coward among others. Quincy Jones wrote the score, which also adds to the film's charm. In the film a professional thief named Charlie Croker (immortalised by Michael Caine) is handed a foolproof plan to steal £4 million in gold bullion from a convoy carrying it between Turin airport and the city's central bank. Croker convinces imprisoned underworld boss Mr Bridger (splendidly played by Noel Coward) to back the scheme and armed with fake data designed to confuse Turin's computerised traffic control system and three Mini Cooper S cars to transport the stolen gold through the paralysed city, he and his gang set to work. After a few setbacks organised by the local Mafia, who don't take kindly to large-scale robberies being pulled off under their noses, the job goes ahead with spectacular success. One of the qualities that makes the film stand out above many other similar films made around the same time is the unbelievable stunt driving of the Mini Cooper S cars, which were piloted by l'Équipe Rémy Julienne. Led by Rémy Julienne himself, the drivers put their Mini Coopers through seemingly impossible stunts during the film. Driving at speed down alleyways, through shopping malls, through subways, across a weir, over the roof of the Turin opera house and most famously of all following a car chase around the roof of the FIAT factory at Lingotto with the ever-present Turin carabinieri, a jump in which all three Coopers leap from one building to the next three stories up. The sequences are simply amazing and were all shot live – not a special effect in sight.

Given such onscreen bravery that entirely chimed with the giant killing reputation of the Mini Cooper S, immortality for both the film and the car soon followed. Almost as though the little car had been canonised, the Mini Cooper entered a kind of motoring heaven in which selected models stood above the rest. Although the human elements of *The Italian Job* are highly questionable (there's a great deal of mid-twentieth-century cheesiness about the film), the automotive pieces are peerless. Far from participating in this sudden interest in a fading model, British Leyland, as the manufacturers had recently been renamed, refused to supply the film company with cars and so they had to buy and wreck their own Mini Cooper S types in the making of this classic. Truly a public relations opportunity lost and symptomatic of the ridiculous state that Britain's motor industry had got itself into by 1969.

As the decades wore on Mini Coopers made the odd appearance in films and TV. In a kind of anti-hero pose a well-worn Swiss registered Mini Cooper was used as a getaway car in *The Bourne Identity*, released in 2002. After some amazing driving stunts around Paris (including a nod to *The Italian Job* when the Mini is driven at speed down a set of steps with a police motorcycle in chase) the car is abandoned in an underground car park.

In 2003, with MINI Cooper production in full swing, Troy Kennedy-Martin reprised *The Italian Job*. Using MINI Cooper cars and aiming straight at the US market, which BMW saw as the main market for their little hatchback, the film was an unabashed plug for the new MINI. A contemporary cast was recruited including Mark Wahlberg as Charlie Croker and Charlize Theron as Mr Bridger's daughter Stella. The slick production won awards and was commercially successful worldwide, particularly in countries where the original Mini Cooper was unknown. However, it simply didn't have the odd British charm and outrageous bravery of the 1969 film and so it has faded from memory whereas the original remains enduringly popular.

Popular British TV series *Heartbeat*, which ran from 1992 to 2010 but was set in the 1960s, featured a green and white 1963 Mini Cooper S (which was briefly owned by the author). Other small appearances on film and TV by the original Mini Cooper come and go, latterly limited to classic car restoration shows, which is natural given the increasing value of the surviving original cars.

Although film and TV were the main arena for appreciation of the Mini Cooper, there are references to Mini Coopers in songs by Madonna and Sheryl Crow among others. In cooperation with Rover, fashion designer Paul Smith launched a self-branded Mini in 1998. Many of the 1,800 examples made featured Cooper engine conversions, giving

Designer Paul Smith created this fantastic Mini Cooper as a promotional item in the 1990s. A calmer version was produced by Rover Group during the latter years of that decade. (*EVO* magazine)

them a bit more power and drivability. Twiggy (born Lesley Hornby), a fashion model from the 1960s, has publicly endorsed the Mini range (including the Mini Cooper) during her long career.

If the world was in any doubt about the cultural impact of the Mini Cooper its presence in the form of prints, mugs, calendars, teapots and even a Chinese-made copy (the Lifan 320) help keep the spirit alive. In addition to the many Mini Coopers still on the road of course.

Chapter 9
Historic Revival: the Classic Mini Cooper

With the burgeoning interest in classic cars from the late 1970s onwards the Mini Cooper was a popular and (initially) economical focus for enthusiasts and restorers alike. Clubs for Mini Cooper owners were formed (such as the Mini Cooper Register) and the value of cars started to rise. A whole new generation of drivers (including the author) was introduced to the delights of Mini Cooper motoring and ownership. Many a previously neglected Mini Cooper was dragged out of its resting place and subjected to 'restoration'. Restoration ranged from a full rebuild by acknowledged experts to a quick blow over and bodge by the average car dealer or owner. It was very much a case of buyer beware when it came to acquiring a shiny looking 'Cooper' and it was not unknown for Minis to pose as Mini Coopers and Mini Coopers to be passed off in the guise of the more valuable Mini Cooper S. Nevertheless, a lot of people had a lot of fun and enjoyed their Mini Coopers even though the youngest of the cars was now more than ten years old.

Along with this revival came new types of motorsport, historic racing and historic rallying. Racing was relatively well regulated in the UK and due to the long-standing interest in racing vintage cars, a historic formula and races were soon put in place to allow post-1950 saloon cars to compete against one another, just as they did in their heyday. The most famous expression of this phenomenon in the UK at the time of writing is the annual Goodwood Revival weekend where Mini Coopers can once again be seen racing on the Sussex track just as they did back in the 1960s. There are other historic racing events around the country and in Europe, which attract a dedicated following.

Ripe for restoration. A structurally sound but dismantled early Mini Cooper such as this makes a perfect project for the brave restorer. All you have to do is find the missing pieces and bolt them on! (Peter Barker)

Smoke grey and Old English white, as shown on this Austin Cooper S, was one of the rarer colour schemes offered by BMC. Discontinued in April 1964, the paint scheme makes this Cooper S a rare beast. Other indications of the car's early origins are the shape of the front apron, which is fully rounded at its outer ends, and the small pointed forward-facing door handles. (Peter Barker)

Above left: By 1968 the Cooper Car Co. works racing versions of the Mini Cooper S were becoming highly sophisticated. Mk2 bodies gave the cars a contemporary look – important when promoting the standard product. (Peter Barker)

Above right: For late 1960s track use 'Rosepetal' alloy wheels and Dunlop racing tyres were fitted to Cooper Car Co. team racing versions of the Mini Cooper S. The fibreglass wheel arch extensions shown were fitted to keep the cars both legal and clean. (Peter Barker)

In rallying the Royal Automobile Club promoted the Golden 50 RAC Rally in 1982 for historic cars. Overwhelmingly popular, somewhat to the RAC's surprise, this one-off event prompted other organisers to create their own events. With the formation of the Historic Rally Car Register in 1984 and the running of the first Pirelli Classic Marathon in 1988, the historic rallying movement took off in the UK and spread abroad. Historic rallies were organised by many motor clubs, some small local events, others national, or as time went on international events with hundreds of classic cars entered. The Automobile Club of Monaco introduced a historic version of their famous Rallye Monte-Carlo in 1998 and it soon grew to an enormous mobile rally festival, with up to 350 classic cars rallying over classic mountain stages in the middle of winter. An enterprising Swiss enthusiast called Raymond Gassmann revived Europe's oldest rally, the Rallye des Alpes, in 1989, running it as a competitive event for historic and vintage cars until 2012. The Mini Cooper was a popular choice of car for historic rallyists, particularly in Britain where cars and spare parts were always available at a price.

The author with Willy Cave at speed in our 1965 Austin Cooper S during a very slushy stage of the 2009 Rallye Monte-Carlo Historique. Wet conditions such as these are a particular challenge to the waterproofing of the forward-facing ignition system on a Mini Cooper. (*MiniWorld*)

The author (blue jersey behind car) discusses a problem with the Tripy GPS technician in parc fermé on the Quay Albert 1er, Monaco, before departing for the Common Run of the 2010 Rallye Monte-Carlo Historique. A wealth of classic machinery and enthusiasm can be seen on this wonderful event. (*MiniWorld*)

Above: The Coupe des Alpes. The Alpine rallyist's most prized possession, this silver cup was awarded to the author and Willy Cave at the end of the 2010 Rallye des Alpes Historique. (Peter Barker)

Left: 977 ARX crewed by the author and navigator Willy Cave on its way to winning the 2003 Rallye des Alpes Historique. This photograph was taken forty years after 977 ARX, also with Willy Cave on board, crashed out of the 1963 Alpine Rally. (Francois Haase)

1965 Morris Mini Cooper S shown here on the Bullnose Rally with the author and Simon Wheatcroft. Disaster struck when a rock punctured the sump, releasing all of the engine and gearbox oil. (*MiniWorld*)

At one time so much money was pouring into historic motorsport in the UK that national motorsport authorities (Stuart Turner among them) worried that contemporary motorsport would wither from lack of funds. This has not happened and historic motorsport has settled down into a healthy minority interest.

Along with the revival of competition opportunities for the Mini Cooper came a welcome second wind for some of the model's most famous drivers of the past. All of BMC's star Mini Cooper drivers from the glory days of the 1960s were once again seen in ex-works cars or replicas based upon them, racing around circuits and demonstrating their skills on the rally stage. For a brief period lucky private owners could compete against the heroes of their youth or even sit next to them in the car competing as a team. Some old Mini Cooper partnerships were revived (such as Paddy Hopkirk/Ron Crellin and Timo Makinen/Paul Easter), and a few new ones formed (Geoff Twigg and Graham Carter among many others). Time took its toll on the old stagers but a new generation of Mini Cooper racers and rally drivers have taken their places and there are some very skillful people to be seen exploiting the handling and performance of their Mini Coopers in historic competition today.

Above left: Veteran navigator Willy Cave fortifies himself with a banana before the 2009 Tulip Rally. Thirty years after his European Rally Championship career Willy had another career as a historic rally navigator including twenty-five events with the author in Mini Coopers. (Peter Barker)

Above right: Geoff Twigg and Graham Carter in a Downton tuned Austin Cooper on their way to winning the 2000 Rallye des Alpes. Their win on this event was the first win by a Mini Cooper since 1967. (Alpine Rally Association)

Peter Jopp (centre) and Willy Cave (right) during the 1970 London to Mexico World Cup Rally. Willy's long career as a navigator was less than halfway through at this stage; he was still competing well into the second decade of the twenty-first century. (*MiniWorld* archive)

As time has gone by the values of classic Mini Coopers have gone up and up. Never the cheapest cars on the road, the Mini Cooper and Cooper S models are now appreciating as valuable classic car investments. In 1961 the average annual wage in Britain was £672 and a new Mini Cooper was priced at £679. Nearly sixty years later the average annual salary in Britain is £36,611 and a restored early 1960s Mini Cooper can be yours for approximately £26,000. In real terms the cars are actually cheaper than they were at launch, although they are no longer bought as daily transport.

A late registered Mk2 Mini Cooper S pictured at Downton Football Club. The Mk2 Mini Coopers were sophisticated cars compared to the earlier Mk1 versions. This nicely maintained example in Island blue and Snowberry white features replacement front seats, an alternative steering wheel and improved lighting. (Peter Barker)

Charming 1966 Morris Cooper S in Tweed grey and Old English white. Valuable extras including a Moto-Lita steering wheel, reclining front seats, a vinyl sunroof, a radio speaker under the rear parcel shelf and 4.5-inch J steel wheels are all visible in this picture. (Peter Barker)

Above: An early Austin Cooper S in Almond green and Old English white at a Downton Works Social Club meeting. Apart from replacement number plates the fixtures and fittings on this car look original. A nice example of a used and enjoyed Mini Cooper S. (Peter Barker)

Right: This Almond green and Old English white 1964 Austin Cooper S was briefly owned by the author. An early car with a single fuel tank, range was limited to 120 miles per fill up. Cars built from 1966 onwards had twin fuel tanks fitted as standard. (Peter Barker)

To keep Mini Coopers running both on the road and in competition during their fifth, sixth and now seventh decades some of the original engine tuners have developed their skills, ex-Downton Engineering employee Steve Harris being one example. A number of newer names have appeared among them including Steve Whitton at MED Engineering in Leicester and Rod Taylor at SMMC in Southam, Warwickshire. Parts supplies and development have been kept alive even in the Mini Cooper's darkest hours by MiniSpares, initially based in London, and MiniSport of Padiham in Lancashire among others. With these and other specialists available, as well as continuing interest in the older models, the future looks bright for the classic Mini Cooper.

Above left: Southam Mini and Metro Centre (SMMC) has been the home of many wonderful Minis over the past thirty years and more. Run by the Taylor family from Southam in Warwickshire, England SMMC is a Mecca for performance Minis. (Peter Barker)

Above right: Ready for the 2011 Rallye Monte-Carlo Historique, the author's Austin Cooper S stands awaiting collection from SMMC. (Peter Barker)

The author (left) at the start of the 2009 Tulip Rally discovers that two of his car's newly fitted rear wheel studs have just sheared. The importance of good quality spare parts cannot be overstated. (*MiniWorld*)

A fine trio of rally Mini Coopers among other competition machinery at the British Motor Museum, Gaydon, Warwickshire. Car shows such as these attract old timers and new enthusiasts alike. (Peter Barker)

Chapter 10
Postscript

Few cars can claim to have changed the world for the better. The Mini Cooper can do so, however, as it offered affordable sporting and highly practical transport to young (and not so young) people throughout its forty-year production life. Originally intended only to compete in motorsport, the Mini Cooper became a motoring icon whose virtues were extolled again and again and whose flaws were pretty much overlooked. To drive an early Mini Cooper and experience just how poor the brakes and synchromesh are is a brutal 'reality check' in today's speech, but even these failings do not detract from the car's magic. The introduction of the Mini in 1959 chimed perfectly with changing aspirations and social conditions in Britain. Similarly, the Mini Cooper in 1961 connected perfectly with young people's desires for excitement and independence while keeping them safe on the increasingly crowded roads of the time. The Mini Cooper capitalised on the virtues of the standard Mini (its roadholding, handling and packaging) and added a few of its own (increased performance and improved interior fittings). For many the Mini Cooper was the ultimate Mini, indeed the ultimate small car of the twentieth century.

As this is written popular opinion is turning against cars and the internal combustion engine on account of the damage it has done to the world's climate. The benefits that individual mobility and sporting performance have brought to the driving public should not be forgotten though. An electric MINI Cooper was announced by manufacturers BMW in 2019, which may prove to be another success in the long story of the Mini Cooper. Whatever happens it is hard to believe that people's desire for personal mobility in a relatively small vehicle that handles well and responds quickly to its controller's commands will disappear entirely.

1962 Morris Mini Cooper 977 ARX pictured in 2006. Over its long life and in various guises, this veteran rally car competed in sixty national and international rallies before retirement in 2008. (Peter Barker)

Appendix 1
Selected Resources

Owners Club
Mini Cooper Register
Formed in 1986 the Mini Cooper Register is the premier car club focused on the Mini Cooper. Based in the UK but with branches overseas, the Mini Cooper Register (or MCR) has hosted an annual get together aimed at Mini Coopers and their owners each June at Beaulieu in Hampshire since the club's inception. Other events are also organised including car runs, tours and regional meetings covering most of the UK and certain areas abroad. All models of Mini Cooper are specifically catered for, as are certain other Mini and MINI models. Membership of the MCR is by subscription to the monthly print magazine *CooperWorld*. (www.minicooper.org)

A collection of works Mini Cooper S rally cars and replicas at the 2010 Family Day outside the MINI Plant Oxford. Built on the site of the former Morris works at Cowley on the outskirts of Oxford, MINI Plant Oxford is a fully automated twenty-first-century production plant. The Mini Coopers shown here, however, were either built in the BMC factories at Cowley or Longbridge in Birmingham. (Helen Hargest)

Magazine

MiniWorld

First published in 1991 *MiniWorld* magazine has thirty years of experience in covering all things Mini and MINI including the Mini Cooper. Currently published by Kelsey Media, *MiniWorld* has had several owners and publishers over the years but continues to thrive and to document the current and past Mini scene. (www.miniworld.co.uk)

Spares Suppliers

www.minispares.com

www.minisport.com

Mini Cooper Tuners and Engineers

Steve Harris Engineering

Barnack, Wilton, Salisbury, SP2 0AW

+44 1722 741575

MED

www.med-engineering.co.uk

SMMC

Unit 1, Baird Park, Brickyard Road, Napton on the Hill, Southam, CV47 8NT

+44 1926 815681

Appendix 2
Images

The extra boot-mounted engine of an outrageous 'Twini' Mini Cooper S built by Neil Preston. Two 1,300cc Cooper S engines, each driving a pair of wheels, gave the Twini Mini Cooper S 180 bhp. The author test drove this car for *MiniWorld* magazine and easily achieved 100 mph between two roundabouts on a suburban bypass. (Peter Barker)

This Mini Cooper S, registered GRX 310D, led a very active works competition life, competing in twelve international races and rallies for BMC including the 1966 Tulip Rally, which it won with Rauno Aaltonen at the wheel. It was then sold to Assistant Competitions Manager Bill Price. The red wheel arch extensions have been fitted to cover wide Minilite alloy wheels finished in gold, which were optional extras supplied by BMC/BL Special Tuning during the late 1960s. (Peter Barker)

The under bonnet scene of
a nicely maintained early
production Mini Cooper S.
The engine has clearly been
modified by contemporary
master tuners Downton
Engineering and has
received improvements
including larger carburettors.
(Peter Barker)

A 1966 Morris Cooper S in
surf blue and Old English
white. Minilite wheels and
a leather rimmed steering
wheel were typical period
extras for the Cooper S. The
presence of rear trailing arm
grease nipple covers just
in front of the rear wheel
suggests a restored or highly
original car. (Peter Barker)

Another shot of a later
registered Island blue
and Snowberry white
Mk2 Mini Cooper S. The
optional wider 4.5-inch
J ventilated steel wheels are
clearly shown, as is the later
type door handle with safety
boss. (Peter Barker)

Twenty-first-century advertising for a twentieth century organisation. The Downton Engineering Works Social Club brings together former employees, car owners and enthusiasts of all types who enjoy the work of master Mini Cooper tuners Downton Engineering (Peter Barker)

Modified Morris Cooper S in Old English white and black shows off some extras. Minilite wheels, a roll cage, a modern driver's seat and the obligatory Moto-Lita steering wheel all indicate competitive intent. (Peter Barker)

Two old stagers, now cherished and displayed at car shows (as here at the Mini Cooper Register's Beaulieu meeting), Morris Cooper 977 ARX and Austin Cooper S 24PK, were once well used on rallies. During the 1963 Alpine Rally they both ran as part of the same BMC-supported team driven by John Sprinzel/Willy Cave and Sir Peter Moon/Brian Culcheth respectively. (Peter Barker)

Pictured during assembly, 'split' Weber carburettors being fitted to Morris Cooper 977 ARX by SMMC in advance of the 2008 Rallye Monte-Carlo Historique. Modified to fit the original inlet manifold, Weber carburettors give improved power and torque over the equivalent SU instruments. (Peter Barker)

Brass banjo bolts on the split Weber carburettors fitted to Morris Cooper 977 ARX in 2008. These bolts have a habit of coming undone if not lock wired in place, as the author found out to his cost. (Peter Barker)

A fine installation of split Weber carburettors on Morris Cooper 977 ARX by SMMC in early 2008. Black metal plate over the speedometer aperture in the bulkhead is to stop fuel ingress into the car's interior. (Peter Barker)

Under bonnet scene from a well-used 1965 Morris Cooper S. The larger 1.5-inch brass-topped SU carburettors are not standard nor are the large diameter engine breathing pipes or plastic splashguard over the ignition. They all help the engine's reliable performance, however. Brake vacuum servo has been removed to aid speedy braking response. (Peter Barker)

Special front seats fitted to 1962 Morris Cooper 977 ARX were originally manufactured by Microcell. Retrimmed using BMC 'polka dot' black and white cloth, they were very comfortable during long distance rallies. Britax four-point harnesses are from later in the 1960s or early 1970s. (Peter Barker)

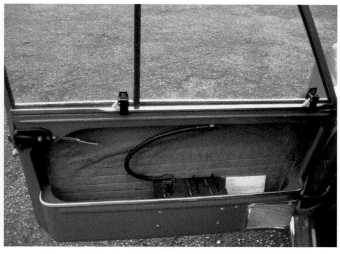

Above left: The interior of a DKG 2C, a 1965 Austin Cooper S as prepared for historic rallies. The dashboard and controls are to a works design straight from the 1960s but the roll cage and front seats are later additions fitted for safety reasons. (Peter Barker)

Above right: Modified passenger's door pocket from a 1965 Austin Cooper S prepared for historic rallies. The switch panel includes controls for the wipers, washers, horn and a flexible map light. Vinyl interior trim has been glued straight to the door skin to save the weight of the standard card trim stiffeners. (Peter Barker)

Three consecutively registered works rally cars, CRX 88B, CRX 89B and CRX 90B, proudly displayed during the Race Retro show at Stoneleigh. Between them these cars competed in ten international rallies for BMC. (Peter Barker)

The Special Tuning four-wheel-drive Mini Clubman created by BL Special Tuning for use in rallycross. Very quickly assembled for use in televised rallycross events and driven by Brian Chatfield, this Mini Cooper S engine car featured permanent four-wheel drive and locked differentials, making it difficult to drive on anything but a loose surface. (Peter Barker)

Works race (left) and rally (right) Mini Cooper S cars from the mid- and late 1960s at Race Retro in Stoneleigh. The classic colour combinations of British racing green/white and Tartan red/white stem from these series of cars. Assorted motoring personalities including Graham Rood, Willy Cave, Bill Price, Robert Clayson and Brian Cameron stand behind the cars. (Peter Barker)

Michael Mark with his Cooper Car Co. racer. A beautiful piece of restoration and vehicle engineering. Just visible are the black inlet tracts for a Lucas mechanical fuel injection set up. This system was never fitted to production Mini Coopers. (Peter Barker)

Works rally car DJB 93B won the 1965 RAC Rally of Great Britain with Rauno Aaltonen and Tony Ambrose as crew. The only Mini ever to win Britain's round of the European Rally Championship, this car was carefully recreated for champion rally co-driver and Mini Cooper enthusiast Phil Short. (Peter Barker)

The end to all fuel feed problems on a competition Mini Cooper: a double-ended SU electric fuel pump. The standard SU pump fitted underneath the rear subframe was notoriously unreliable. (Peter Barker)

L'Affair of 1966 (the disqualification of the works Mini Coopers and other leading British cars from the Monte Carlo Rally of that year) caused a controversy between Mini and Citroen DS/ID owners that seems to live forever. The flamboyant pink Citroen ID 19 of Warren and Jean Chmura is seen here racing Mini Cooper 977 ARX at Llandow Circuit in a timed competitive test. (*MiniWorld*)

Head-to-head, Mini Cooper vs Citroen ID 19. The story of how the tiny Mini Coopers beat the mighty Citroens in the 1966 Rallye Monte-Carlo and were then disqualified is a sporting legend. With hindsight the Mini Cooper's headlamp dipping system was pretty close to the edge of illegality, but was that ever really the point of *l'affair*? (*MiniWorld*)

Creative use of brackets to support auxiliary lamps on the Monte Carlo Rally-winning Mini Cooper S of 1965, AJB 44B. BMC Competition Department's mechanics and fitters could manufacture parts as needed to prepare the works Mini Coopers for their next rally. (Peter Barker)

An excessive number of driving lights adorn the front of the 1965 Morris Cooper S of Bill Richards and Graham Carter at the end of the 2017 Rallye Monte-Carlo Historique. The plastic cups on the windscreen wipers are non-functioning additions. (Peter Barker)

The Mk2 Mini Cooper S of the author and Willy Cave awaits the start on Lake of Geneva, 2005 Rallye des Alpes Historique. (*MiniWorld*)

The interior of Morris Cooper 977 ARX in 2006. Plenty of non-standard equipment is visible as the car was dedicated to rallying from new. The front seats, roll cage, dashboard and steering wheel are all upgrades. Instrument binnacle has been turned upside down to give the single Weber carburettor a little more clearance in the engine bay. (Peter Barker)

Boxy Mk2 Mini Cooper S sits next to swoopy Jaguar awaiting scrutineering in Geneva before the 2005 Rallye des Alpes Historique. (*MiniWorld*)

Under bonnet shot of a very early production Austin Mini Cooper. This restored car has had many minor modifications but retains its Lucas C40 dynamo. (Peter Barker)

The full boot of Morris Cooper 977 ARX. In addition to twin black fuel tanks, a black vinyl tool bag, green jerrycan, red warning triangle plus towropes and jump leads are all visible. Green bag with BMC in white lettering is a Competitions Department fuel bag donated by works co-driver Paul Easter. (Peter Barker)

Engine bay of the author's modified 1965 Morris Cooper S in 2008. The larger brass-topped SU carburettors, alternator, engine breathers and modern relays are non-standard items fitted to aid performance and reliability. (Peter Barker)

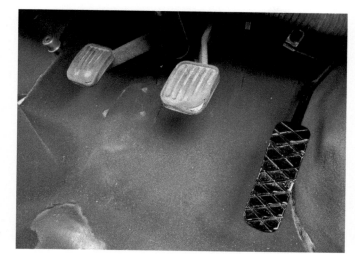

The well used pedals of 1965 Austin Mini Cooper S DKG 2C. The extended throttle pedal was used for 'heeling and toeing' between throttle and brake to ensure smooth gearchanges at speed. (Peter Barker)

Mini Cooper S 3.5-inch J steel wheel with original 1960s Dunlop Weathermaster SP44 fitted. Items like these are fine for displaying at car shows but as they are now fifty years old and should not be driven upon. (Peter Barker)

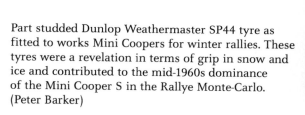

Part studded Dunlop Weathermaster SP44 tyre as fitted to works Mini Coopers for winter rallies. These tyres were a revelation in terms of grip in snow and ice and contributed to the mid-1960s dominance of the Mini Cooper S in the Rallye Monte-Carlo. (Peter Barker)

Vintage Rallye des Alpes competitor's plate fastened to the parcel shelf of the author's rallying Mini Cooper S. Original items such as this are highly prized by enthusiasts. (Peter Barker)

Above left: 1965 Austin Cooper S DKG 2C pictured with some of its period rallying kit in 2010. BMC Tartan car rug and Lucas snow shovel accompany BMC fuel bag and vinyl grille muff. (Peter Barker)

Above right: Rally kit stowed on the rear seat of 1965 Austin Cooper S DKG 2C. Secure stowing of kit inside a rally car is vital if it is not to come loose and cause injury in the case of an accident. (Peter Barker)

1965 Austin Cooper S as prepared for historic rallies by the author. Many works-inspired modifications went into this successful car, which won its class in the 2011 Rallye Monte-Carlo Historique and won outright in the 2010 Rallye des Alpes Historique. (Peter Barker)

Dashboard detail from 1965 Austin Cooper S DKG 2C. This modified car was specifically prepared for rallying by the author. An extensive additional wiring loom was required to supply the various additional instruments and electrical functions. (Peter Barker)

Interior detail of 1965 Austin Cooper S DKG 2C at the start of the 2011 Rallye Monte-Carlo Historique. The instrument in front of the navigator is a Halda Twinmaster mechanical trip meter. The lenses mounted in front of it are to magnify the rather small display of the Twinmaster so that navigator Willy Cave can read it when strapped into his seat. (*MiniWorld*)

Pulling into a service halt with spare tyres ready to fit on the roof rack of our Mini Cooper S. The author with Willy Cave at the 2009 Rallye Monte-Carlo Historique. (*MiniWorld*)

The Mini Cooper S of the author and Willy Cave looking clean and shiny at the start of the 2010 Rallye des Alpes Historique. Note the postman's red rubber bands holding the lamp covers in place and the raised rear edge of the bonnet to allow heat to escape. (*MiniWorld*)

Clerk of the Course and former Director of Motorsport for Austin Rover John Davenport (in the red jacket), with competitor Ben Stebbing and journalist Franca Davenport, examine the front end of the Barker/Cave Mini Cooper S during the 2010 Rallye des Alpes Historique. White brackets at the rear of the car are for a quick lift jack to aid speedy servicing. (*MiniWorld*)

The author conferring with journalist Franca Davenport during the 2010 Rallye des Alpes Historique. (*MiniWorld*)

A blatant bit of Mini parking outside the Hotel Baveno Dino during the 2010 Rallye des Alpes Historique. The open boot lid displays a well-packed interior. (*MiniWorld*)

Mini Cooper S in the lead. The author with Willy Cave clocking out from the first control of the third day ahead of a cavalcade of lovely sportscars. 2010 Rallye des Alpes Historique. (*MiniWorld*)

The author with Willy Cave at speed in their Mini Cooper S during the 2010 Rallye des Alpes Historique. The battery of auxiliary lamps were unused during this daylight-only event. (*MiniWorld*)

Morris Cooper 977 ARX with the author and Willy Cave during the 2007 Rallye des Alpes Historique. Strapped on Perspex headlamp covers are to protect the glass from flying stones. (*MiniWorld*)

Above: With navigator Willy Cave relaxing the author motors on during the 2007 Rallye des Alpes Historique. The roll bar inside the car is a modern fitting on the grounds of safety. (*MiniWorld*)

Left: The author looking glum and navigator Willy Cave pose at the end of the 2007 Rallye des Alpes Historique. We had just learned that due to a marshall's error we had lost our Coupe d'Or, the golden Alpine Cup awarded for a zero penalty score each day of the rally for three consecutive years. (*MiniWorld*)

Our Mini Cooper S receiving the traditional bunch of tulips at the finish of the 2009 Tulip Rally. Not a successful event for Willy Cave and myself but enjoyable nevertheless. (Tulip Rally)

Disaster for John Sprinzel and Willy Cave (standing to the right of the road) just outside Castellet-St-Cassien in the French Alps when the steering column came loose from the rack. Despite this setback Morris Cooper 977 ARX lived to fight another day. (Terry Mitchell)

The author having a cup of coffee during a session of ice driving on a frozen Finnish lake tutored by Rauno Aaltonen in 2008. The MINI Cooper is fitted with fully studded tyres suitable for the conditions. (Rauno Aaltonen)

Dancing on ice. The author reverse flicks a MINI Cooper S on the ice of a frozen Finnish lake while passengers wave during tuition by Rauno Aaltonen. (Rauno Aaltonen)

The author at speed in a MINI Cooper S on the ice of frozen Lake Tahko in Finland. After tuition from Aaltonen Motorsport increased confidence and speed were achieved. (Rauno Aaltonen)

The author with twelve-year-old son Robin demonstrating 977 ARX at the Chatsworth Rally Show in 2008. This was 977 ARX's final appearance in my hands before being sold to collector Patrick Walker. (Neil Burgess)

Replica 1963 Alpine Rally plate for works Mini Cooper 977 ARX. Plates such as these were fixed to the front and back of each car in international rallies during the Mini Cooper's heyday. Today they are highly prized as souvenirs. (Peter Barker)

Three of the best! Two Austin Cooper S and one Morris Cooper in rally trim pictured at the British Motor Museum, Gaydon. The central upswept exhaust was a popular modification for competition Mini Coopers as it gave increased performance and avoided damage to the pipe when disembarking from ferries. (Peter Barker)

Originally owned by rally privateer and bon viveur Sir Peter Moon, works supported Austin Cooper S 24PK competed on several international rallies of its time including the 1963 Alpine Rally and the 1964 Manx International Rally, where it suffered a serious accident after becoming inverted on a stage. This historic car was carefully restored and is displayed at car shows as seen here. (Peter Barker)

A relic. The original T bar for tightening wheel nuts as rescued from the wreck of 24PK by Peter Valentine after the 1964 Manx Rally. Red painted bars either side are later tools of an alternative design. (Peter Barker)

Above left: An idyllic Alpine scene at a control during the 2010 Rallye des Alpes Historique. Entry shows a wonderful collection of classic cars for our Austin Cooper S to compete with including two Bentleys, a TR3 and an Austin Healey. (Peter Barker)

Above right: Waiting at a time control during the 2010 Rallye des Alpes Historique. Our Mini Cooper S just edges in front of the Triumph TR3 of Ben and Katy Stebbing as it did during a highly enjoyable and very close week-long battle. (Peter Barker)

Willy Cave and Mini Cooper S surrounded by a superb Swiss Alpine view at the finish of the 2010 Rallye des Alpes Historique. (Peter Barker)

Colin Taylor of SMMC refits an SU carburettor during the 2005 Rallye des Alpes Historique. (*MiniWorld*)

Struggling through the snow on 10-inch wheels, Morris Cooper 977 ARX with the author and Willy Cave on board during the 2008 Rallye Monte-Carlo Historique. (Phillipe Fugier)

A frozen Mini Cooper S. A beautiful study of the author's rally mount during the 2010 Rallye Monte-Carlo Historique. (Lara Platman)

Idyllic mountain scene showing the author and Willy Cave in 1962 Morris Cooper 977 ARX during the 2006 Rallye Monte-Carlo Historique. Door No. 1 was awarded by the Automobile Club of Monaco in tacit recognition of the fortieth anniversary of the disqualification of the winning works Mini Coopers in 1966. (Gerard Brown)

Swedish rally driver and twice winner of the UK's RAC Rally Harry Kallstrom with a Mk1 Mini at his home in 2007. (Peter Barker)

Veteran navigator Willy Cave gives a cheery smile from our Morris Cooper S with the author behind the wheel during the 2008 Lombard Rally. Having competed in international rallies since 1955, Willy seemed to know most of the minor roads of Europe. (*MiniWorld*)

Off into the mud of another stage on the 2008 Lombard Rally in our well used 1965 Morris Cooper S. Willy Cave and I competed on four of these events and enjoyed their straight-forward although gruelling nature. (*MiniWorld*)

90 left round a bush during the 2008 Lombard Rally. The Mini Cooper S was a competitive car in the British forests so long as the going didn't get too rough for its tiny wheels. (*MiniWorld*)

1965 Austin Cooper S of the author and Willy Cave swings round a corner in a French village during the 2010 Rallye Monte-Carlo Historique. The car has lost its chromed plastic wheel arch trim, a common occurrence on rallying Mini Coopers. (*MiniWorld*)

The author with Willy Cave in their modified 1965 Austin Cooper S during the 2011 Rallye Monte-Carlo Historique. In this final year of its competitive life DKG 2C was running on 12-inch wheels and modern winter tyres courtesy of MINI Plant Oxford. (*MiniWorld*)

Alastair Vines with Peter Moss in their ex-works Austin Cooper S CRX 89B chases an Opel during the 2011 Rallye Monte-Carlo Historique. Having competed in six international rallies with BMC, CRX 89B then had a second life as a historic rally car in the Pirelli Marathons of the 1980s and on the Rallye Monte-Carlo Historique. (*MiniWorld*)

Mini racer and engine builder Bill Richards with Professor John Morrow in their MiniSpares-sponsored 1964 Morris Cooper S during the 2011 Rallye Monte-Carlo Historique. A colourful pairing, Bill and John competed in several editions of the rally with mixed results. (*MiniWorld*)

The author with Willy Cave battles Morris Cooper 977 ARX against Italian mounted opposition on Serre Chevalier ice racing circuit during the 2007 Rallye Monte-Carlo Historique. A large silver cup came our way after this excursion. (*MiniWorld*)

Brian Culcheth (left), Paddy Hopkirk (centre) and Andrew Cowan(right) with a works Mini Cooper S outside British Leyland Motors. All three drivers raced Mini Coopers for the factory both in Europe and in Australia. (*MiniWorld* archive)

Snow and slush for the 2008 Rallye Monte-Carlo Historique but the Morris Cooper of the author and Willy Cave remains sure footed on the exposed tarmac. (Phillipe Fugier)

The author looks nervous before the start of the 2011 Rallye Monte-Carlo Historique. Months of planning goes into a serious attempt at an international event such as this. The driver can terminate his or her chances of success in a few seconds. (*MiniWorld*)

The author and Willy Cave receive their time at the end of a stage of the 2005 Lombard Rally. Tough but slow in comparison to the opposition, this car had already competed in the 1994 Network Q RAC Rally and 1996 Rallye Monte-Carlo by the time it came into my hands. (Lisa Thornton)

The author and Willy Cave prepare for the final night's mountain circuit in their 1965 Austin Cooper S. 2011 Rallye Monte-Carlo Historique. (Lara Platman)

Helmut Artacker (left) and Rauno Aaltonen (right) get ready for the final night's mountain circuit of the 2011 Rallye Monte-Carlo Historique in their 1969 Austin Mini Cooper S. (Lara Platman)

The cold light of an early morning falls on the 1965 Austin Cooper S CRX 89B of Alastair Vines and Peter Moss in parc fermé, Valence, during the 2011 Rallye Monte-Carlo Historique. (Lara Platman)

Mini racer Bill Richards (left) and Professor John Morrow (right) look calm as they arrive in Monaco in their 1965 Morris Cooper S. 2011 Rallye Monte-Carlo Historique. (Lara Platman)

A fine line up of Mini Coopers from Wales at the Paris start of the 1964 Rallye Monte-Carlo. Crews are (from left to right) Frank Rutter and Des Tilley, Norman Harvey and Denis Cardell, and D. T. Nicholas and Mr Hughes. (Denis Cardell archive)

The author with Willy Cave weeping a little fuel in our 1993 Rover Cooper 1.3 SPi rally car at Weston Park during the 2005 Lombard Rally. The Rover Cooper, although tough, proved uncompetitive against modern opposition. (*MiniWorld*)